T0333876

'*In All Weathers* is a beautiful book, a shimmer of unexpected ways of seeing and experiencing the world, shining with detailed insight and attentive understanding. Wild, oppressive and inclement weathers have found a wonderfully gentle champion in Matt Gaw – these are explorations to delight every walker and refresh any reader.'

HORATIO CLARE, author of *Heavy Light*

'Matt's vivid, personal journey through weather will inspire you to welcome and embrace even the dullest, dampest, shiver-inducing-est of conditions. Uplifting and full of wonder.'

LEV PARIKIAN, author of *Taking Flight*

'A brilliant, bracing, elucidating book. Wonderfully researched and written.'

STEPHEN RUTT, author of *The Eternal Season*

IN ALL WEATHERS

A Journey Through Rain, Fog, Wind, Ice and Everything In Between

MATT GAW

Elliott&Thompson

First published 2024 by
Elliott and Thompson Limited
2 John Street
London WC1N 2ES
www.eandtbooks.com

ISBN: 978-1-78396-773-5

9 8 7 6 5 4 3 2 1

A catalogue record for this book is available
from the British Library.

Typesetting by Marie Doherty
Printed by CPI Group (UK) Ltd,
Croydon, CR0 4YY

MIX
Paper | Supporting
responsible forestry
FSC® C171272

For my family and my friends

CONTENTS

PROLOGUE

WEATHER. UNWEDER.
Suffolk, August 2022

It is late afternoon and my wife Jen and I are in the garden. The heat is dirty and still; the air warm as blood. We lie on a rug that we have pulled half into the shade and look up into a pale but cloudless sky. I'm looking for swifts. It has been a couple of days since I have noticed them scything and flickering around the houses in our street, screaming at the sun. I wonder if they have gone, and if that means the weather will finally break. Although it must be around 5 p.m., the sun is still fierce. I can feel the skin on my face blurring with sweat as I scan the skies again. Jen is squinting. She says the light feels strange, like when you've screwed up your eyes too tight and then, when you open them, everything is bleached out. As if the world has become an old photo.

I cover my eyes with my arm and think about the weather. The temperature has been stuck on at least 30°C for two months now. Ceaseless. Heavy. At its worst, it is like the heel of a hand on the top of my head. It tightens the skin around my collarbone until it pinches; presses down with hard fingers on the bridge of my nose; makes my skull feel as if it is overflowing with something gloopy, thick and hot. It is a heat of bright, sickly colours. Split custard yellow. Curdled white. Jags of red. I can't remember a summer like it. There have been heatwaves, yes, but this? The UK's first red warning for extreme heat came on a glowering July day, when the air and land trembled under a greasy thumb-streak of haze. The temperature reached a record 40.3°C. It was not warm. It was not beach weather. It was a rail-buckling, road-melting, spit-sizzling assault.

July 2022 will subsequently be named as the driest on record for East Anglia, the driest since 1935 for the rest of England. Now it is August and the consequences of the prolonged heatwave are all around. Many of the trees have dropped their leaves. In the hedgerows, the sloes and berries have shrivelled before they could swell. Ivy snaps between fingers like burnt crisps. The rivers have retreated. In places, the flow of the Lark and the Linnet disappeared upstream. The wet ditches, the ponds, have all gone. The only water comes from the farmers' pumps that arc in long hissing tuts across fields full of burnt crops and cracks wide enough to fit your hand in. On our walks – taken only in the evening and with decreasing frequency – we have noticed dead birds. Blackbirds, thrushes, tits, rooks, jays and magpies. Some are victims of thirst and starvation, but all are signs that something has stopped. The saprophytes — those soil-dwelling organisms that feed on the dead and decaying — cannot function in the moisture-free soil. The creatures that fall do not rot as they should, but stay intact, along with knotty strings of fox scat baked white as bone.

Even now, with the temperatures back to around the seasonal average, it still feels unbearable. The heat squats in rooms long after the sun has gone down. It puffs off furnishings and furniture like dust. The air creeps like lava that steams and swells as it meets our mouths and lungs. The temperature, the endless bloody sun, is all we talk about now. It is on our lips, our tongues, in our dry throats.

TV meteorologists explain the conditions in terms of air masses and cycles: high pressure is 'dominating' and pushing Atlantic fronts carrying rain to the north-west. This, they say, allows temperatures to build elsewhere. The words make it seem as if this is OK, that what we are seeing is part of a normal natural cycle. Nothing to worry about. Nothing to worry about. Nothing to worry about. But, lying here, I can't get it out of my head that it doesn't feel right. It doesn't. The truth of it lurks like a shadow on a hospital scan. There is something wrong. This is the unweder of the Old English, weather that is so extreme it seems to have come from another climate, another world. It makes me realise that not only do I miss the usual contrary weather of

Britain, but also that for some time now I've been overlooking so much of it.

As a child I used to be fascinated by a weather house that sat on the windowsill at my grandparents' home. It looked like a thatched cottage, with walls covered in pale pink shells the size of fingernails. It had two doorless openings, both containing a simple model of a person. Under one door, in shaky white paint, was written the word 'SUNNY'; under the other, 'WET'. As if by magic – even when I was told about the interplay between catgut and moisture, it still felt like magic – the sun would draw the smiling man into the open air. Rain, drizzle, an approaching storm, or even a sniff of fog would send him indoors and draw forth the other man from the darkness. He crept forward with his hat pulled down tight as if he were disgusted at the thought of putting a single chipped toe over the threshold.

It is a sentiment that many of us – in many cases, unconsciously – share. The culture of the UK, a place founded on wind-blown migration and the navigation of storm-whipped seas, is undoubtedly weather-soaked. Yet, it seems to me that it is also incredibly lopsided. For the great majority of the population, our livelihoods and day-to-day existence are now long divorced from the practicalities of seed planting or the need for good visibility in Dogger, Fisher, German Bight, and we seem to have forgotten the fundamental importance of those rhythms. Our weather is now too often judged as simply good (sunny) or bad (anything else). The rain, the cold, the wind are things to be endured with chins down and collars up or, if at all possible, avoided altogether.

It's an easy narrative. The sun boosts feel-good hormones, serotonin levels, and gives us vitamins. The sun is life. It nourishes us, helps us wake, helps us sleep. From an early age, as soon as a fist can hold a yellow crayon, we see the sun as a symbol of happiness. We bathe in it. We worship it. We follow its light. But what if we could find equal joy in other weather? Learn to appreciate the refreshing beauty of the rain; the wild freedom of a whipping wind; the dazzling reflections of light on ice; the otherworldly nature of fog. What if, rather than staying indoors, we could go out and embrace all this so-called unpleasant weather? After all, if the sun has become inclement, glaring down on us without mercy, could other weathers be luminous and nourishing if only we open up to them?

So, this year, I am determined to redress the balance, to look again at what is our most widely accessed experience of the natural world and realise that not only can it be beautiful and sublime, but it can also be fun.

It's an important point. Many of my childhood memories – some of them now as brittle as old photos – are centred around just *being in* weather: the first drops of rain from a thunderstorm; pulling a red sled through a snow-smothered woodland so empty it was as if a spell had been cast; a wind that pushed us laughing down a hill and then rocked our caravan so hard I could hear my dad swearing through gritted teeth; a sea fog so thick we could only hear each other's voices as we ran to the waves. I want to recapture those feelings, to make new memories for my own family – to rediscover the kind of childlike wonder that makes the world suddenly seem so big, new and exciting again.

I resolve not just to brave inclement weather but to actively seek it out and enjoy it: to explore and understand where our weather comes from, the ways it can so dramatically transform the light, textures, shapes and colours of a landscape, and the effect it can have on us – our behaviour, our mood. How it has inspired poets and artists, seeped into our language, and fundamentally shaped our way of life on these isles. How its wildness makes it a rare part of nature over which we have no control. I will revel in the sheer variety of weather that washes over this archipelago, and use it as my lens to observe the world afresh. After all, when our death lies sly in the long grass of unnumbered days, we cannot live our life only in the sunshine of spring. Life needs to be grabbed with both hands. Because to experience weather, to see and feel how its patterns change, is to notice the rhythms of the planet, to see how the different facets of the world interconnect.

I will follow so many that have gone before in taking down the weather in notes and diaries. I will fill my life and home with the elements: rainfall in the bedroom, dew points in the bathroom, hoar frost and the north wind in the kitchen. It won't be a universal analysis of weather, but rather a personal story of walking, swimming and reflecting on a year of weather. It will be a way of recalibrating myself and reminding myself to take time to notice. Perhaps it may be a useful stepping stone to help others do the same.

So, let the rain pierce the skin like splinters. Let the snow form crystals in your marrow, let the wind circle and rush into your ears until you hear the blown tide of your own blood. Dress for it. Don't dress for it. Close your eyes to it, open your lips and arms to it. Throw open the doors, windows and soul to the sublime wildness of weather.

RAIN

At times rain is a devastating disruption that explodes into our lives, transforming rivers to destructive torrents and sending floods into our homes and businesses. But mostly it is simply seen as an annoyance; an inconvenience that stops play, ruins weddings, picnics, camping trips, sports days and hairdos. Dull, dreary, miserable days filled with grey cloud, drizzle and mizzle. When was the last time you deliberately went outside to feel the rain on your skin?

By avoiding rain, we've forgotten how to appreciate it – how it falls, how it feels, how it affects the land. Our knowledge has been relegated to the wet and wild nomenclature of old: the dabbly rain that sticks to the skin in Suffolk or the moor-gallop of Cumbria and Cornwall where the rain moves in quick-moving sheets across high ground.[1]

Perhaps it is easy to want to rethink rain now that its absence has stretched on for week after dusty week, but I find myself longing to experience and enjoy it, rather than view it grimly through a window. I want to relearn and relive rain in all its forms: frontal rain that falls when cold and warm air meet; orographic rain caused by air passing over high ground; rain that comes down so hard it takes the breath away. I want to run outside when it explodes out of the blue, to walk through the showers, deluges, downpours and drizzles that leave the world glistening and renewed.

BREAKING. PETRICHOR. STORM.
Suffolk, August 2022

In our house we always sleep with the soothing sound of the rain. *Google, play the sound of a storm.* We ask for it without fail. First, a distant peal of thunder and then a wet tapping that builds quickly to a torrential white noise. My daughter does it too. Every night you'll find two localised rainstorms rattling around upstairs. Damping down the day, making the house, the bed, feel that much more cosy. We drift off in a safe, rain-ringed harbour. But tonight there is to be a third storm.

We hear it coming in the early hours. The deep, belly-rumble of thunder growing to a vicious crack that sounds like something terrible is being broken. We talk quietly, slipping in and out of sleep, plotting the distance of the storm by counting the seconds between the sheet lightning that flashes white around the edges of the blind, and the corresponding hollow boom of thunder. One, two, three, four, five, six, seven, eight, nine, ten. Divide by five. Two miles. We wait, staring up into the darkness. Flash. I drum the seconds out on my stomach. One, two, three, four, five. Boom. One mile. The air is changing. Becoming charged. *Closer*, we whisper. *It's definitely getting closer.*

We have been waiting for this for weeks. For something, somewhere to shift and for the pressure to be relieved. The storm will be, we hope, the reset switch. A turning off and on again that will make the weather behave in a way that is more, well, normal. That will bring an end to what feels like two months of ceaseless, almost violent heat.

A couple of days ago, on a breathless evening when outside was marginally cooler than in, rain had begun to fall from a lumpy bank of cumulonimbus. Jen and I stood in the garden and looked up until our necks hurt, expecting a downpour, for the rain to turn thick and heavy. The patio slowly darkened, but you could still walk between the drops without getting wet. There was almost enough time for the stone to dry before the next drop fell. This wasn't yet to be the relief we'd been waiting for.

The smell was there though. You know it. You'd know it anywhere: petrichor.

The word was first used in 1964 by researchers at the Australian CSIRO science agency to describe the yellow-coloured oil, which is responsible for the scent, that was released from rocks after they had been steam distilled. In

Greek, *petra* means 'stone', and *ichor* refers to the golden fluid that flows through the veins of the immortals of Greek mythology. The oil is a combination of plant secretions (signals to halt root growth and seed germination during dry weather) and chemicals released by soil-dwelling bacteria. Some people are said to have a nose for petrichor. So much so they can actually smell when it is going to rain, as the higher humidity causes the pores of rock and soil to fill with moisture and push oils into the air. But the smell is strongest when the rain finally arrives. As raindrops, falling at 9 metres per second (about 20 mph), explode on dusty or clay soil, they trap air bubbles, which are then thrown upwards and out, taking aerosols of scent with them.

For me the odour is sharp, almost animal. It is a smell that bubbles with memories: dust and straw from the rabbit hatch; a single ice-cold drop on the back of my neck; the zing of the rain on the black lid of the barbecue; running down the side of the house to shelter in the garage. It is standing on a concrete floor that is cool to the point of dampness and ringed with oil from someone else's car while listening to the clatter of heavy rainfall on the half-closed metal door.

There is an excitement with petrichor that I'm sure is linked to anticipation, to relief. We have our personal memories, like mine of the freedom of childhood. But maybe there's a deeper, older, shared memory too. A memory of a time when our needs were tied more tightly to rain, when it was wished for.

On this evening, the dog seemed to smell it too. Whether it was the rain she was excited by or the change in pressure, she had barked and chased up and down the garden – a skipping, see-sawing sprint, topped and tailed with dramatic pounces and turns that send dead grass and dust flying. She rolled on her back, wriggling her shoulders down into the earth the way she does to collect any scent she deems delicious. Her legs kicked as she rolled before she flipped back over and did another lap of the garden, her ears pressed back against the roundness of her skull. She stopped and stuck out a lolling tongue. A paw raised. Unsure again. I held out a hand. Nothing. The rain had stopped. The drops on the patio dried. The humidity ratcheted slowly back up. Inside the heat hadn't shifted at all. It stood silent and dark in every room, like a guest who had outstayed their welcome.

The next day I spoke to my parents, who live about a forty-five-minute drive away. Their phone line was crackling the way it does when it gets damp. For years engineers have tested and probed. Dug up the path outside, replaced cables, sucked their teeth and made test calls, but still, when it rains, the phone line crackles and spits. Gobbles up whole words. They had rain, they say, my dad on the phone and my mum shouting from the back. The high street flooded. I know exactly where it will have been. I can see the water pooling at the bottom of the valley down by the line of houses by the Mill, the parade that now houses more betting shops than grocers and bakers, the black timber-framed pub where *Lovejoy* filmed in one exciting week in the late 1980s.

It used to be the river itself, the Colne, that crept into homes and businesses, but the floodgates stopped that. Now it is the dryness of the land that causes flashes of brown water to rise up to people's knees. The soil, starved of moisture, has become hydrophobic – it repels rather than absorbs. The water stays on the surface and gathers speed and force as it courses over concrete, brick, paving slab, road and gardens that have been hammered flat by the sun. My dad says he had to turn around by the fire station as he drove into town; the water was too deep for cars. I told him that they stole our rain. The line crackled and fizzed in response. The voices are swallowed.

This night though, the rain will finally arrive in full force. We slept again. We must have done, because when I open my eyes my son is here and so is the storm. Standing in the darkness, he is talking quietly but urgently. His room is at the top of our narrow house. He says it is too noisy, too bright in there. The hair on his legs is standing up on end from the static. The lightning flashes, once, twice, three times and the thunder rolls almost at the same time. Hammer on tin. The anvils of our ears shake. The storm is right above us.

I lift the sheet and Seth gets in, shimmying on over to Jen. The realisation that he's scared, that he still needs us, still wants us, is as welcome as the rain. He is a teenager now. On the cusp of becoming. He has increasing independence, views, tastes and desires of his own. His life, as it should, is beginning to unfurl from our own. The hand holdings are becoming rarer, the kisses on the cheek are more quickly taken. But tonight he is a child again, his slim back cuddled into my wife's stomach. His head, with its loose curls, fitting under her chin like it did on that very first night when every part of him felt like something impossible: a wonder, a miracle. I listen to them breathing together. The rhythm of them. The shallow gasp as the lightning flash comes just a heartbeat before the roll of thunder. There is no time for counting now. The storm is right above us, the speed of light cannot outrun the thunder. The rain is so loud it sounds as though water is coming into the house. The gutters have given up. Rain sluices down windows and walls. The building feels like an old wet dog that is done with shaking. I get up and Jen asks what I'm doing. Her voice is soft. Sleep heavy. Cloud thick. 'Are you going out?'

I am. I hadn't really thought about it, but I am. I have a strange yearning for the freshness of the rain, the end of this bloody heat. I get dressed, then half undressed again. There doesn't seem much point in trying to protect myself from the rain when it is hammering down like this. Anyway,

I want to feel it. I want to wash the dirt and dryness from my pores.

In the end I step outside wearing nothing but shorts and an old pair of espadrilles whose soles are fraying into yellow bristles. I am soaked almost immediately. The rain takes my breath away. Stings my bare shoulders, which I raise and round as if stepping into cold water. It feels as if the rain is needling through skin and beating onto my bones. I breathe and breathe, taking deep gulps – the air is not scented now, it is clean as a Sunday night hair wash – walking down the path away from my house and turning left to follow the water that is sliding in sheets down the road, bunching up behind car wheels, washing away a month of dust, death, dog dirt and fag ends. The drains take great, gurgling, air-filled gulps, but even more water flows over them, around them. It is about 6 a.m., but a pre-dawn darkness holds, pressed into place by the heaviness of clouds that have locked together to obscure their fibrous edges, their kilometre-high anvil-like tops. Under the streetlights I can see the rain falling in thick bolts, momentarily turning to sparks of light. The ferocity is incredible. Thousands of 20-mph collisions. Thousands of tiny explosions on bare skin.

There is another quick flash of lightning. It reminds me of the man who used to live in the house directly opposite who would play video games into the early hours on a giant projector. I would sometimes wake to see light and shapes flashing silently into our room. Now there is thunder too, juddering from different heights but at the same time directionless, filling up everything with its sounds. It is not a uniform noise like the recordings we listen to at night – that safe, throat-clearing rumble. It is low-flying aeroplanes; it is a heavy suitcase on wheels, dragged over the loose floorboard in an upstairs room; it is standing under a concrete road bridge; it is the roll of bowling ball on polished wood; it is explosive bomb blasts that rattle bones and close your eyes like the snap of a snare drum. They build and ride over each other.

We talk of thunder and lightning, but it should really be lightning and thunder. After all, it is lightning that starts it all – or, if we're being really accurate, it is ice. In school we are taught that when warm air rises, it cools and condenses to form water vapour. But if the updraught is quick, really quick, the water vapour will form cumulonimbus clouds in under an hour. The warm air will continue to rise inside clouds that at their peak can stretch for 16 kilometres upwards, the water droplets freezing and combining as ice crystals. When the droplets are too heavy to be supported by the updraughts they fall within the cloud, picking up a negative static charge as they rub against smaller, positively charged ice crystals. The negative charge accumulates at the base of the cloud, while the lighter ice crystals gather at the top, forming a positive charge. Like the balloon that sticks to the wall and the ceiling, the negatively charged droplets are attracted to Earth's surface, to other clouds and objects

– including the positively charged ice particles. When the attraction becomes too strong, a discharge of energy is emitted as lightning. The air is heated to 20,000°C – over three times hotter than the surface of the sun – causing it to expand at such speeds it creates an acoustic wave. A sonic boom. It is the sound of the air snapping back, of energy shaken off, of the weather rebalancing while all the time the rain adds its own endless hiss. I've read that, at ground level, a clap of thunder registers at 120 decibels, the point at which sound becomes painful to human ears. It is rock-concert loud, ten times that of the asphalt-biting crunch of a pneumatic drill.

At the end of my road, the lights of one of the bungalows are on. The windows are flung wide, like eyes stuck open, staring onto water that has flashed, gritty and grey over kerbs to fill driveways and lap against red-brick walls. The junction, with its traffic island, its fallen beacon, has been smoothed away to leave an expanse of water that almost reaches to the petrol garage on the main road. I stop and watch the patterns on the surface caused by the falling rain, dimpling and bubbling. I dangle a toe. Submerge a foot. Keep going. Right now, away from the main road, it feels as if I'm walking with the storm. If anything, the rain is getting stronger, beating down so hard it hurts my collarbone and forces my eyes closed. Drops fall, fat and heavy, so hard that they jump back into the air again. It is falling down and up.

But there is something affirming about being in the rain. Something I hadn't expected. I feel the rain. But somehow the rain also seems to be feeling me. The rain touches every part of you physically. It makes an unthinking map of you, highlights the space that you are taking up. Each drop forces you into some corporeal *cogito*, to say *I am here, I am exactly here at this exact time*. This weather, this place, this time. It sharpens the thinking by reducing the world to crystalline pinpoints. It forces you to stop and take notice, to become more aware of your own being, of your movements through the world with its insistent wet touches.

I stop by the main road where cars are now shushing slowly through the floodwater. I stand watching in my shorts until the water reaches my ankles, until the rain begins to ease and gaps open up in the thunder, the lightning sprinting northwards. Then I walk home slowly, feet sloshing, full to the brim with a sensation that feels aerated and sweet as wine. I breathe deliberately, in through the nose and out through the mouth, appreciating the way the combination of early morning and heavy rain makes the day seem clean and fresh. The air is no longer solid, cloying. There is a lightness, a sense of shock, of discharge. The earth has changed, has been restored, by rain. It has made the act of movement, of living, pleasant again.

By the time I'm close to my house, the thunder is distant and the rain has found a more gentle rhythm. The sound of water rushing to drains has softened to the kind of gurgle-drip you would expect in a spring thaw. On a chimney pot, three houses up from mine, a jackdaw is calling. A strange little 'well, fuck me' laugh. In the neighbour's front garden, the sparrows are chattering inside a hedge that offered some shelter from the downpour.

Seth has decamped to the sofa when I get in. Up in the bedroom, Jen is almost back to sleep. She says she enjoyed it well enough where she was, thank you very much.

We talk in low, sleep-beckoning voices about the sound of the storm, about Seth's reaction, the way he had folded back into us. She remembers how at her primary school there would almost be hysteria as the thunder rumbled overhead. The kids would say it was the clouds knocking together. God moving the furniture. She turns towards me and I wrap my arms around her. I put my hands on her back and ask if I'm cold to the touch. She mumbles, presses her own hand to my chest. Her fingers are splayed, their tips pulsing with heat.

You know it was a hot summer, she says, because I'm so warm. I'm like a Victorian house. It takes a lot to heat my bricks.

I smile in the curtained room, place a foot against a calf. Through the window there is a breeze. The air is sweet, cool and finally moving. The heat has broken.

The rain continues for the rest of the day. The fury, the desperate nature of it left with the storm. It falls instead with an ease, like a long-distance runner hitting their stride. Eating up the miles. A radar map shows a multi-cell thunderstorm made up of a cluster of storms – each probably lasting only twenty minutes – with a squall line of dozens of miles. I set the screen to animation and watch how the column of rain poured north over Sussex, London and then Suffolk. The head of it is a mad scribble of white tracer marks, each representing 300 million volts of lightning.

The national news reports the downpour, picking out the top of the drops. Bury St Edmunds recorded 62.8 millimetres of rain – 2½ inches in old money – in just three hours. The monthly average is 55 millimetres and there is too much for the parched earth to swallow. It fills roads and stands in fields. I think about phoning my parents, to say that this time, this time, it was us who won the rain.

SHOWER. BLANKET. LIGHT.
Suffolk, September

The weeks that follow are full of showers. Proper showers, with downpours heavy enough to soak you to the skin in a matter of moments. One arrives as I run a circuit around town, the rain so heavy it makes me gasp, the water forming a film over my eyes that I can barely blink away. It fills my mouth. It soaks into earphones until the music stops and all I can hear is the pump of my own blood and the open-palmed applause of the rain.

The town centre roads and paths aren't slick with wet; they are submerged. I run with knees held high, guessing where kerbs are, where the slabs dip and rise. The movement of the water is amazing, gushing from all angles; across the cobbles of the car park and the street by the churchyard, tumbling down towards the old Shire Hall and the Court and the police station in inch-thick sheets. It is water that demonstrates the lie of the land in a way that is invisible in the dry. It says this is the shape of things, this is how water and light move.

I used to think that 'shower' was a degree of light rain. A step up from a drizzle (with its drops of less than 0.5 millimetres), but several rungs below a deluge. A category apart from 'pissing it down'. While the nomenclature of rain is varied, there are really only two types: blanket rain and showers. Blanket rain is widespread. It comes from stratus clouds, which are usually part of larger frontal systems that can cover hundreds of miles and can turn entire days the colour of chewed paper. Showers, on the other hand, come from cumulus clouds, formed by convection (the cooling of warm air as it rises), and whether they are cats-and-dogs heavy or spitting light, they are short-lived and localised.

Showers are possible at any time of the year, but they are much more likely during the settled summer months. Throughout the day, the sun heats the ground and the surface air temperature starts to build. The heat is not equally distributed. Darker areas, urban locations, heat up more quickly and when there is a 2- to 3-degree difference air begins to rise. This thermal, this bubble of air, will cool as it rises but will keep moving while it is warmer than the surrounding air. Eventually, the air will condense enough to create shower clouds. Topography is crucial. Showers are especially likely to form over hills where air has been forced to rise and at the coast where cooler air from the sea replaces air that has been heated up on land.

The one that I have found myself running in started quickly, almost out of the blue, as if a tap had been turned on.* But of course, there would have been warning signs if I had only been paying attention, or known what they were. There would have been an increase in the number of clouds, the darkening of their colour. The cloud bottoms would have become ragged. There might have been the dark shreds of pannus, a fractus cloud that forms under a precipitating cloud. The Cloud Appreciation Society describes them as a 'sort of cloud version of hoodies, killing time outside McDonald's on a Saturday night',[2] but one that tells you it will rain in five minutes. Maybe there would also have been

---

* Rain coming from cloudless skies is known as 'serein'. The name is thought to come from the French *serein*, meaning serene or clear. This kind of rain, which usually takes the form of a few spots or a light drizzle (typically after dusk) has been explained in various ways. One explanation is that the rain is being blown from a distant cloud by strong winds at high altitudes or that cloud droplets are evaporating at the same time as rain falls.

virga clouds, formed from cloud bases when rain falls but doesn't reach the ground, their frayed edges trailing earthward like dark, carded wool.

What I do know, is that right now the water, the sheer mass of water, slopping and spouting off concrete and brick, is unbelievable. Past the Abbey Gates the drains bubble into low fountains. Shoppers shelter underneath scaffold boards, using hands and carrier bags to protect their heads from the water that still dribbles through. Others keep walking, moving fast with their shoulders hunched up towards their ears, T-shirts slapped tight to skin.

As a child I would try to dodge the rain with my friends. We would debate techniques, discussing the benefits of going slow, being exposed for longer, against running at full pelt. In 2012, writing in the *European Journal of Physics*, Professor Franco Bocci suggested that it was a complex issue and the answer depended on an individual's height-to-breadth ratio as well as wind direction and raindrop size. His advice? 'The best thing is to run, as fast as you can – not always, but in general.'[3]

The rain is still hammering down as I go past the Abbey Gardens, over the road and up Northgate. I'm surprised by how much I'm enjoying it. I feel that same lightness I did when the weather broke. My watch is telling me that the last mile has been my fastest. I've been throwing myself forward into the rain, pressing myself into it. I wonder if I've been running to its rhythms rather than the silence of my drenched headphones. By the beautician's, with its driveway of ridged concrete, the water comes in sluices that press hard against the ankles. A woman is standing on a bench. Underneath her the water rushes on, picking up dust and grit. She smiles. Waves.

'I'm soaked,' she says, 'but I want to save my shoes.'

The song on my headphones kicks back in. Plays two notes, spits and is gone.

The clouds, dense, dark and seamless, are quick. Quicker than me. By the time I am home I am at the edge of the shower, on the cusp between heavy rain and nothing at all. I stop and rock forward onto the balls of my feet. I can feel the water in my trainers squeezing through my toes, the slight chill of my T-shirt clinging to the centre of my chest. Delicious and fresh: cold fabric on hot skin, like two fronts meeting.

Jen has been saying for a week, maybe more, that autumn is on its way. In the evening when we watched our eldest play football and the shadows rushed cool and long from their running feet; when the apples in the orchard behind our house began to thunk into the grass; even when she rolled up her trousers in the garden to catch 'the last of the sun'. Right now the early-evening sun is shining through rain-drops that are still fat and heavy. It's as if the rain is a lens that makes the light visible. There is definitely autumn in the light. It is unmistakable. The rain is butter coloured. Gilded. Emulsified. The air honey sweet.

The next day the water is gone. The motion of it is still there though. There are mackerel-striped ridges of silt and soil. Groynes of grit around car tyres. Tiny ghosts of deltas that fan out from the alleyways where I walk the dog.

HEAVY RAIN. FRONTAL RAIN. TRANSITIONS.
Seathwaite, October 2022

The peak of Seathwaite Fell, the northern ridge of Great End, has been reduced to a pale ghost. A dark line that soon will disappear completely, erased as easily as if it were a pencil sketch. The clouds that have tracked up its seaward side are now beginning their descent, as though they are re-enacting the scouring slide of long-ago glaciers that once formed the Borrowdale valley. In an hour, maybe less, this valley, walled in by its sharp crags, veined with milk-white gills and gullies, is in for a proper soaking.

The hamlet of Seathwaite, where I'm standing, is no stranger to getting wet. Seathwaite's average yearly rainfall is 3,552 millimetres, making it the most rain-soaked habitation in the UK – well in excess of the UK average of 1,163 millimetres. That is why I had to come here. It's one thing to enjoy the rain when it comes after the heat and sweat of a long summer but I wanted to immerse myself in real rain, to be in the wettest place I could find; a place rain calls home.

The volume of water is due largely to the hamlet's location in the UK. It is westerly, near the coast, and damp air blows in off the Atlantic. It feels the effects of the fronts more keenly than more eastern regions. But also the low-pressure systems, which often predominantly track across northern areas of the UK, can influence rainfall totals.

There are other more local factors at play too. Weather is specific to place; it is tethered to it. The weather that happens where you are can happen only there. The weather here can happen only here. And Seathwaite is a lesson in hydrology: the very landscape shapes the weather and in turn that weather has forged the character of this drenched land. It is a living, breathing diagram of what is known as orographic or relief precipitation. Hunched at the end of the long finger of the ice-cut and river-wetted Borrowdale Valley, Seathwaite is surrounded, almost walled in, by sharp-edged crags. When moisture-laden air comes in from the Atlantic, it is forced up and over a volcanic ridge that includes England's highest peak, Scafell Pike. The air cools as it rises and condenses into rain. And what rain. When it comes down on the lee side, on the slate tiles of the terraced cottages and the farm, on the cobbles, on the backs of sheep and the heads of shepherds, it does so with biblical fury. It fills rain gauges. It fills rivers. It fills roads and fields. It, as they say round these parts, hosses it down.

Two days ago there had been torrential rain across Cumbria. The highest rainfall was here at Seathwaite, where rain gauges recorded 9.9 centimetres in just twenty-four hours. Yesterday, when I explained to the hotel manager that I was coming to walk in the rain, she had told me about the deluge. Said that she hadn't seen anything like it. The Derwentwater breached its banks. Sheep were swept away by flash floods and cars left stranded – up to their tyre arches in water. 'It came down so hard it hurt my face,' she said. 'It felt like it was made of glass.' I remembered the sting of the rain in my hometown, the dimpling of puddles, the sensation of being almost coloured in by the rain.

Despite its remote location, Seathwaite is a place that thousands of walkers go through each year to reach the peaks. They come here to follow the trail that leads towards Scafell Pike – not a neat standalone mountain, but the tallest tip on a ragged ridge of fells. From the air it looks a bit like a fossilised shark tooth, erupting from the soft gums of the valley. The hamlet itself is tiny, essentially a farm and a neat row of squat cottages, made to seem smaller still by the fells that rear up behind them. The loom and lour of Seathwaite Fell. The heavy brow of the peaks beyond. I have a flash of concern: walking here could be a very different prospect from walking in Suffolk. Just how fast does the water come off the fells?

To the right, under the skinny, white water of Sour Milk

Gill, is a large slate-rubble barn. Across a narrow street of smooth cobbles there is what looks like another farm building, given over as a camping barn, and terraced to three houses whose roughcast walls have been painted a brilliant white. The gates to the front gardens are closed. The chimneys are smokeless. There is little sign of life: no lights shine from the thin panes of the sash windows. But they don't look like holiday homes. Against one upper window is a line of blue cuddly toys. Outside the door of another hangs a see-through mac, ready to be grabbed. The same is true of the farm buildings. I notice now there are wax jackets and cagoules all hung within easy reach. There is a way of life that is hardwired here: always, always expect rain. There is a dog barking somewhere on the fell. The noise of it runs around the rocks until it's swallowed by clouds. It feels as if the air is getting wetter. The slates are slick and black. Even the light, diffused through heavy clouds, is low and watery.

I follow the sign that says Styhead and walk onto a streamside gravel track that wends into the valley. Away from the shelter of the buildings it is the wind I notice first. The south-westerly, which is bringing in this front of rain, is gusting hard. There are times when it holds you mid-footstep, snatches at clothes, before shouldering past and down the fell. Another walker is descending. He is on his way back to the car. Having spent a night wild camping on the fells, he says he is keen to get home.

'I wouldn't go up if I was you,' he adds. 'The rain is coming in and the wind is bad enough down here. Up there it's probably an eight.'

His glasses are beaded with water. His eyes grey and serious. I don't want to tell him why I'm here, or how I've come precisely because of this 'bad weather'. I don't tell him that I've been tracking it for days, watching it move across the Irish Sea like a shoal of fish on a trawler's echo-location; seeing it split then come together again like a hand balling into a fist. Instead, I say that I'm not planning on climbing. Just a stroll. But he's already moving off. He throws a hand back above his head in farewell and crunches away down the track. I watch him go, seeing the wind putting a hand to his backpack and pushing him up on to tiptoes, forcing him every now and then into a skittering run. I turn back towards the peaks and rock on my heels. The fizz of rain is in the air, the excitement rubbing off on me.

I realise how glad I am to be out. To be opening my legs out. To feel foot against rock. It has been a while since I've been able to make space for walking for any longer than a few hours.

It's not a complaint. It's just life. The trade-off for the closeness of family and the security of employment is a lack of personal time. The tightening of orbits. Busy schedules that demand all our attention, so we get out of the habit of noticing things going on in the wider world around us, including weather. Before I started taking notes, you could have asked me what it was like last week, perhaps even yesterday, and at best I could have provided just the broadest brushstrokes. When can you pinpoint the last time you experienced a cloudy day with average temperatures? Even though we talk about weather constantly, unless it is extreme – unless it breaks our infrastructure, screams at us, roars above the din of everyday life – we rarely really notice *being in it*.

Not noticing is a human quality. The rest of the animal kingdom appears tuned in, but our minds seemed to have evolved not to see their surroundings. The environment, our environment, is a backdrop against which the interesting things in our lives take place. Perhaps it is a survival technique in a hectic modern world. We think about the big picture, not letting the brain become mad with spinning leaves or obsessed with the changing cloudscape, full of raindrops, fogged up. But it is a way of living that comes at a price. Writing in *The Once and Future World*, J. B. MacKinnon suggests it is this coping strategy that could be behind the phenomenon of shifting baseline syndrome – where the state of the natural world we experience when we are young is taken as 'normal'. Memory, he says, 'conspires against nature'.[4]

As we focus on the things that are critical in our lives, we are blind to gradual change around us. We adapt to the new conditions and any memory we do hold of the original state of things adapts with us. All the time we continue to believe that it is impossible we could have not noticed something with our own eyes, a condition that psychologists have described as 'change blindness'. And as MacKinnon says, 'If you don't believe that you are capable of missing significant changes in a scene, then you won't heighten your awareness in order not to miss them – which means that you probably will.'[5]

I wonder if weather can be a way back in. A model of how we should experience the world. If we can just notice how it feels to move through rain, the way the wind sings off objects around us, maybe we can start to notice, well, everything else. Perhaps our weather can, in some small way, teach us to see again.

Now that the path is tacking deeper into the valley, I can see around the dome of Seathwaite Fell, to the ridges behind and the peaks of Great Gable, and the wall of Great End, the most northerly mountain in the Scafell chain. From the south it is simply another peak, another uprising. But from the north it appears as an immense mountain, with an imposing north face rising above the waters of Sprinkling Tarn. The great, high ridge of Allen Crags. Above them all is a solid wave of cloud. It rears, bulges and teeters, sends rags of spindrift over the edges. I have never seen an avalanche in real life, just on film. But I am reminded of that. Of a sense of bundled-up power. Of snow moving so fast it merges with the air to form a rushing white powder. It's hard not to give the movements of weather intentionality. To see the clouds as something gigantic, hauling themselves over the ridge. Perhaps in part it's a way to avoid being overwhelmed by the sublime scales of weather. By telling ourselves it is directed at us, it is coming for us, we give ourselves a sense of importance in the world, a role beyond that which has been cast. We stop ourselves being consumed by forces so much greater than us, beyond our control.

From this perspective, I can see that the underside of the cloud above the ridge is rough and unravelling. There is a lot you can tell from a cloud's bottom. It marks the height at which temperature is cool enough to condense the water vapour in the atmosphere – the dew point. Since the dew point is, generally, consistent in any one location, the base of a cloud is uniform and flat. But while rain is created by clouds, rain is also a cloud creator. Rain is cold and when it falls, the air underneath the cloud is cooled, leading to more condensation and the growth of new cloud that curls under the first like fraying, grey fangs. It looks a bit like wool that's being teased apart for spinning. It even has that greasy lanolin look. A fleece that needs a hot wash. The light up there is doing strange things too; pulsing and shimmering as the rain falls on the highest slopes.

I stop, then walk, stop again and stand with my head tilted back to watch the clouds move and change. Growing and fading like breath on a mirror. I raise my phone and try to capture it on photo and then on video, but all of the images seem impossibly flat, as if it takes a human eye, a mind, to capture the experience. It is like trying to capture a laugh in letters. In fact, later, when I try to write down some notes, when I try to explain to my children what it was like to watch a rainstorm slide down the fells towards me, I will struggle to find the words to make the experience come alive, to make it move and breathe. Strangely, it is only when listening to music that I can get anywhere close to recalling it, to conjuring that feeling of swooping, dancing life. It is only certain combinations of notes that make my heart beat with the rain's rhythm. Maybe it is because weather and music are both immaterial and material at the same time, both able to influence how we feel and how we experience the world.

It won't be long now before the rain reaches me. The air is thick with moisture. When I was young, if the clouds darkened but the rain didn't fall, my mum used to say it was 'trying'. Hands out. Looking up. As if she was feeling the intentionality of the clouds, the straining concentration of them. It's trying. It's definitely trying. It wants to rain.

A movement on the grey of the ridge. There is a large bird flying up towards the rain. I think at first it is a heron. It is hard to get a sense of perspective against the steep strew of rock. It seems to be the right size. The wings are a grey of rock and cloud. Limestone with wingtips of wet slate.

The dark grey of storms. It banks, sticking close to the almost vertical face of the fell and then sliding down with wings outstretched. It isn't a heron; of course it isn't. I look at the wing width, the amount of Indian ink that tips the five spikes of its primaries. It peels off from the rock face and flies to the valley bottom with shallow, gullish flaps. There is a calmness to it, the authoritative way it takes up space, that sets this bird apart. That whispers predator, that writes hen harrier, hen harrier, hen harrier across my brain in hot sparks. Later, when I look up if rain impacts on their hunting and breeding (it can reduce the amount of food males provide for chicks), in my mind's eye it is close, almost within touching distance, rather than on the edge of what I can comfortably see. The thickness of the body. The yellow brightness of its eye.

The hen harrier lands by the slate-coloured water of Grains Gill. I lose him then as he hunches among the rock litter and the stone-flow of the water. Definitely a him, there's no mistaking that pale pigeon grey, blue as cigarette smoke. I keep watching, scanning the fells for more movement. I hold a thorn from the bush that clings to the edge of the path, press it against the soft pad of my thumb. Look at berries the colour of bitten lips. Down by the water there is an opening of wings. The hen harrier rises quickly, gaining height before it opens its wings out and glides, flying with the flow of the gill, back towards lower land and Seathwaite.

The trail leads up and down, winding deeper into the valley until I reach the picturesque arch of Stockley Bridge. The path is solid. Made of rocks sunk into the earth. But there are loose stones too, so it almost feels as though you are walking along the bed of a stream. The water of Grains Gill – shallow, clear and carrying the grey of the sky – licks white over boulder and slab as it squeezes its way through pinch points and runnels in the rock. But it's easy to see what the water can do. To see how it can grow. Under the bridge I can see where rocks, as big as a fist, have been rolled into a line on the riverbed. Downstream, the earth has been chewed from the hillside where I had been walking. I can see the thorn tree where I stood watching the harrier. When it rains here, things change pretty quickly. It's something I've heard again and again.

There are no trees to slow things down, to block and deflect water with branches and roots. The water hits, skids and flashes off rock. It charges down the fells and into the river. It becomes a wild, desperate thing, thumping under this bridge and galloping towards Borrowdale with stones in its pockets. In the floods of August 1966, after a long period of heavy rain, the bridge itself was swept away by the flood waters. I imagine it's not the first time. I can't believe it will be the last.

The path is steepening, becoming single-file. The rocks looser, more easily rolled under foot. There are runnels every few paces. Designed to carry the water off the path and over the side of the gill, joining the waterfalls that cut crow's feet into the hillside. There is sedge, grass nibbled down to the root and sheep shit scattered like giant, loosely formed blackberries. I can see on the fells each side of me that the rain is moving in bands of light. The rain is slipping down the fell in sheets. Greasy ribbons. Undulating. Curving. Rippling. Bands of light and dark. Striped like mackerel. Moving in roving, quick-eyed, hungry-mouthed shoals.

Closer.

Closer.

And there is a sound too. I hear it now. A growing *shush* that reminds me of the murmuration of starlings I watched last year in the valley fen near my home. A mass of birds that expanded and contracted in a billowing black pulse of wing beats and fluttering hearts. The air itself shook with them. It fizzed. As if they were the lung from which everything poured and . . . and then I am not looking at the rain, I'm not listening to it or thinking about anything, I am in it. There is a moment of shrinking away from it, of lowering my head, squinting; all the things we do to make ourselves physically smaller and escape the sensation of rain, before I remind myself that I have come here for just this: frontal rainfall. There is a relief that bursts out of me in a laugh. Because it is raining, and however silly it might seem to drive for six hours to experience rain, to drive six hours to not find rain would have been far worse.

31

Different regions have different terms for rain. A whole lexicon of wetness that expresses not only that it is raining but how. In my home county of Suffolk there are dags of rain (showers) and dabble rain that makes the air moist and sticky. There are leasty days, when the weather is dull and wet, and the smurs of fine mist.* But in Cumbria there are no half measures. It seems in the Lake District it is either yukken it down, hoyin' it down, hossing it down or not. Out of all the names for rain that I have heard, my favourite is one that is used in both the Lakes and in Scotland. Stotting means to rain so hard it bounces off a surface. It rains up and down, just like it did on my run in Bury St Edmunds. Stotting, somewhat beautifully I think, is also a synonym for pronging or pronking; that stiff-legged leap that antelopes do to show how sprightly they are (and therefore hard to catch) to potential predators.

I stop with my back against a rock; pull down my hood and lift my face so I am staring at the fells. They are still crowned with clouds. I can feel the coldness of the rain on my face. I stick out my tongue like a child. I remember how in primary school we used to try to drink the rain – standing with our backs against the brown-skinned Portakabin with our faces upturned, tongues cupped and waiting. We did it for rain, for hail and for snow. Shrieking and talking

* See *Rain* by Melissa Harrison for a countrywide list of words for rain.

in throaty gulps. It must have been around that time, in the early to mid-1980s, that *Newsround* started reporting on acid rain and I stopped sticking my tongue out. I thought of those American forests where the trees had sickened and the lakes contained nothing but acidic water. I thought of limestone buildings that started to melt like sugar cubes and imagined what sulphuric and nitric acid could do to a pink slip of a tongue.

Looking back, and in the light of what we now know about the climate crisis, acid rain seems almost charmingly nostalgic. Like an early horror film where the monster never looks quite right. But there are still jump-scares contained in our rain. In 2020, a report published in the journal *Science* revealed that microplastic particles equivalent to as many as 300 million plastic water bottles are raining down on the Grand Canyon, Joshua Tree and other US national parks. Researchers said that across eleven remote locations, more than 1,000 metric tonnes of microplastics had travelled through the atmosphere like water particles. In 2022, another study, published in *Environmental Science and Technology* by scientists from Stockholm University, went further still. Rainwater everywhere on the planet is unsafe to drink due to levels of PFAS.* Even in places such as Antarctica and the Tibetan planes, PFAS were found

* Per-and polyfluoroalkyl substances – chemicals used in a range of consumer products.

to be fourteen times higher than allowed in US drinking-water guidelines. Ian Cousins, lead author of the study, said, 'We have made the planet inhospitable to human life by irreversibly contaminating it now so that nothing is clean anymore. And to the point that it's not clean enough to be safe.' But of course, it's not just humans that drink the water.

A study published in *The Science of the Total Environment* in 2023 suggested that PFAS-triggered conditions in wildlife included suppressed immunity, liver damage, reproductive and developmental problems, bowel disease and a whole lot more.[6] And it found that almost anywhere you looked, these 'forever chemicals' had polluted our rainwater.

There are advantages to stepping out in inclement weather that go beyond understanding our landscapes in different conditions and lights. Each year, 15.8 million people visit the Lake District, with the highest number choosing the school summer holidays of July and August. During those times, the fells become bright with sun and walkers. But in the off season, when it rains, they are gifted empty to anyone who wants them. Apart from the descending hiker near the start, I haven't encountered a single soul on the trail above Seathwaite. Here there are just the sheep for company. They are gently stupid things, with wide muzzles and eyes that give them a kindly, mildly surprised expression. An 'Oh, what are you here for?' look as they amble off ahead, or skitter behind rocks.

The Herdwicks, or Herdy, are not bothered by the weather. Their fleece is thick and comes in nimbus-cloud grey. It is full of protruding bristles that protect them from downpours and blizzards and is heavy enough not to be parted by the winds found in the fells. I've heard it said they can even survive being buried in snow for days at a stretch. That they'll eat their fleece and wait for the diggers to arrive, greeting their saviour with that same even, benevolent stare. Herdy are also, whether through long experience of rain or something hardwired and instinctive, expert shakers. They can shake and chew and shit at the same time.

The Herdwicks are an integral part of this place. A solid fixture like the bridges, the drystone wall. The root word of the breed's name, *herdvyck*, 'sheep pasture', is recorded as far back as the twelfth century. The story goes that their lineage is linked to the Norse and they have been here since the tenth or eleventh century. They certainly know the land. The Herdy were traditionally managed in a way that means they stick to certain parts of the fell, with the location of their own heaf passed from ewe to lamb. The sheep play their part in shaping – or destroying – the land too. Their nibbling suppresses vegetation and the wildlife that depends on it; removes any tree seedlings that might have otherwise taken root, providing cover and a way of slowing the rain-water that flashes off the fells.

These sheep take no notice of me as I carry on past them. The rain moves in ribbons, like a flock of something living. Striped and flashing. Light and dark.

I've been thinking about how weather can be so tied up with emotion, how it is used as a medium to express the human experience. As an English teacher I often find myself talking about rain. We use it to judge tone and mood in writing. OK, class, it is raining, what does that suggest? We use it in our own writing as a literary device. A pathetic fallacy. Our skies weep. Raindrops stick to windows and slide down the glass, like tears. Our rain is metaphor and simile for mood and misery. It is damp and dour. Soaking and sombre. It is the pantomime villain that speaks with a sibilant lisp. It is the rain on our parade. The piss on our chips. But I've found little sadness in the rain. In fact, it feels like the opposite. There is a lightness, a joy in being in the rain. A sense of something fundamental, of connection.

When I told my brother that I had been out in the rain and was coming here, he reminded me of an old teacher. I hadn't thought of her for ages. Her long dark hair with its badger flash of white. The rose-coloured crystal she wore around her neck and clothes that smelt of joss sticks. She spoke about chakra and chi. And when it rained she said she would stand outside and feel totally alive. It sounded New Age and twee at the time. But science backs her up.

Because when the clouds burst, there is something other than water in the air. Negative ions are atmospheric molecules that are charged with electricity. They are most abundant around places such as rivers, beaches and mountains, where air molecules are broken up by moving water. They are found near breaking waves, by waterfalls and they are there, too, when it rains.

Negative ions, which are breathed in, transferred to blood and brain, have been linked with biochemical changes that impact on mental health. A 2013 review of scientific literature published between 1957 and 2012 found that negative ions could have a significant impact on people with depression. Even low levels of exposure – just half an hour – could have therapeutic effects on those suffering from seasonal affective disorder. A study published in the *Research and Behavioral Sciences Journal* suggested that treatment for mood disorders with NAI (negative air ions) is 'in general effective within effects almost equivalent to those in other antidepressant non-pharmacotherapy trials'. In short, while we might look out of the window and associate wet weather with gloom and *noir* and misery, being out in the rain can actually boost our mood. It might sound counterintuitive – and certainly long stretches of dreary, grey and rainy days that last until you forget what the sun looks like can be a mood dampener – but thinking back to my walk in that heatwave-breaking downpour and the shower I ran through, I felt that same up-swing in serotonin that I do when I swim in cold water. I felt more focused. Calmer. Happier.

The rain of the Lake District certainly did not dampen the spirits of the Wordsworths. Writing in 1822, in *A Guide Through the District of the Lakes in the North of England* – a collection of notes, directions and descriptions intended to be used by tourists and residents – William finds beauty in the rain. 'Showers, darkening or brightening as they fly from hill to hill, are not less grateful to the eye than finely interwoven passages of gay and sad music are touching to the ear.'[7]

In her diaries, Dorothy also notices the potential for an experience of rain to be uplifting, to be something that can be enjoyed. She walks in 'soft rain'. She noticed how 'the sun shone while it rained, and the stones of the walls and the pebbles on the road glittered like silver'.[8]

Many of the artists of the Romantic age composed their work in the field, writing, drawing or painting outside. John Constable was known to have sketched in the open air and in the rain on more than one occasion. Both William and Dorothy Wordsworth would take inspiration from being exposed to rain and showers. After sheltering from a downpour at Alfoxden, where Dorothy described how the 'withered leaves' of the hollies had 'danced with the hail-stones', William composed 'A Whirl-blast from Behind the Hill', where everything jumps, sings and dances with elvish, almost supernatural life. It is probable that Wordsworth, like Constable, would finish his sketches or draft out his thoughts in the comfort of his home. But even then, as Alexandra Harris points out in *Weatherland*, he is described as writing with the windows open.

For me, one of the things I adore about the Romantics is the idea that weather is not something to be shut out or ignored. The weather is not even to be looked at, regarded as if it is somehow separate to the human body and the act of living. Rain, like all the other elements, should be felt.

What seems to have really excited the Wordsworths though, at least as far as it is possible to tell from their writing, is not so much a single state of weather, but the moment of transition and transformation.[9] That specific point in time when the attention is captured by drama and the brain cannot help but notice. A shift from the loom of cloud to the sudden downpour. The cessation of the rain and the breaking-through of the sun. The changing of the light that feels like taking a breath.

By the time I stop for a break, the clouds have overtaken me and sunk into the valley. The rain will have reached the hamlet now. It will be hammering into the collecting cans of the weather station. I place a hand over the top of my tin mug to stop the rain plinking into my tea. The sandwich that was made the night before, collected in the early hours from a dark and cold hotel kitchen, has turned damp in my pocket. I eat it quickly, noticing how the valley seems darker. Not in a miserable, mood-reflecting kind of way, but the colours seem more definite somehow. The rocks black as sea pebbles, the green a harder, more lustrous shade.

The rain is beginning to form its own pathways down the fell. It dashes hard off the land. The sound of the rain is meshing with the larger flows of water: the falls, the gullies, the gills. I wonder how many of the paths I have been following are actually desire lines made by water. I am walking in both old rain and new.

In Suffolk there seems to be such a clear separation between earth and sky. They are so far apart, like a child's drawing where the land is a green strip at the bottom, the sky a line of blue at the top, holding birds and a crayon blaze of sun. Between them both an acre of paper. But here the sky and land are jumbled close. Rock to cloud. As I walk again, up steeper paths now, chuckling with water that tumbles down, turning stones, dissolving sheep shit, I feel as though I'm in the clouds, reaching the rain before it even falls. It always feels as if there should be more architecture to clouds when you're consumed by them, that there should be a lining, a tangible skin to them. As though they should be containers from which water leaks, rather than an aerosol, a cold spray of visible liquid droplets.

I try again to video the movement of the rain, to capture the fish-shoal flicker of it. To show the billow and skud of cloud over the ridge, to record the glug of rain-water over rock and stone. I wish that I could draw, that I could sketch out the shape of the landscape and hatch in with pencil how the rain has transformed it: the change of shadows; the interplay between cloud, crag and water; to make how I feel, sitting here in this moment, into something physical and lasting. Would it even be possible to paint in these conditions?

The going gets tougher as I continue up. The rocks now are slick with water. I worry about slipping, falling, about twisting something vital and getting stuck. I imagine being the focus of a local news story where an idiotic tourist when too far in the rain. I turn right over a bridge where Ruddy Gill tumbles down into Grains Gill. There is a cascade and the air is full of spray. It would be a stretch to call it a roar, but it is loud enough to make you raise your voice if there were anyone here but sheep to talk to. It slides and rushes, bubbles over slabs of rocks. I hold the railings tight and think about how lower down the water would be building up under the old pack bridge.

I decide it's probably time to turn back. It's a long drive home and I worry the conditions are going to get more treacherous. But, I argue against myself, I wanted rain, I've found it. I should stay and appreciate it in all its wild glory, even if it does get a bit hairy. I change my mind. Then change it again. Walking up and down, then turning on my heels, muttering to myself.

In spite of my concerns, though, I feel good. The rain has washed away the cold I'd been suffering from for the last three days. The water on my skin has warmed to the temperature of blood. I wonder how different the experience would have been in winter, when the rain would be needled with cold. Would I be so open to getting wet? I think so, yes. I would definitely need a better coat, better boots, some waterproof trousers. Billy Connolly said he hated weathermen 'who tell you that rain is bad weather. There's no such thing as bad weather, just the wrong clothing, so get yourself a sexy raincoat and live a little.' But then again, maybe it's just a mindset. I swim in rivers throughout the coldest months, so why not step outside in the garden for more locally sourced rainwater?

I keep going for now, following the path around to Sprinkling Tarn. It is a name of lightness, but today the water seems heavy: clear but dark as lead. The tarn is heart-shaped with a rocky outcrop that is almost an island at its furthest tip. The kind of island you could swim to, launch yourself off. I think I can see where the path goes, skirting around to Sty Tarn but I finally decide to turn back. Part of it is because my sense of direction is terrible and I'm afraid of getting lost, but also I want to see how the landscape has changed in the rain. I want to have a good view of the valley, to understand how this place forms rain and is shaped by it, and looking at the map, that view would be screened if I keep going. It is a decision I know my wife would hate.

She dislikes to-and-back journeys, she always wants the efficiency of a circular route, the variation of it. I can see the set of her jaw, the slight rise of an eyebrow at the idea of turning back.

If anything, it is slower going on the way down. I walk on my heels to avoid slipping. The paths aren't just wet, they are now overflowing with water. I am walking in streams. The runnels that were dry on ascent are now over-topping. New routes have been formed over grass, everywhere you look is water, all heading down, all looking for the least resistance, all moving as quickly as it can. Even my boots are running with water. There are tides pulling from heel to toe. I wonder what it must have been like a few days ago. How quickly must rain travel to carry off a sheep?

A shepherd is moving a flock above Stockley Bridge. He has two dogs. One black and white, the other black. There is a leanness to them. Tongue lolling, stomach curved into ribs. They are all sleek muscle and speed compared to the wobble bobble of the sheep travelling back into the fells where the rain boils down into the water of the gill. I cross the river again and walk past where the shepherd has left his quad bike at a pinch point on the rocks. Closer to the farm, the cows have travelled back for shelter. They cling to the walls, shielding their flanks in single file. Their dark eyes wet. Their noses wetter still. The houses in the hamlet are crouched against the weather. Stone shoulders raised. There is a truck on the cobbles with its engine purring over.

In a crate in the back is another sheepdog, chin resting on paws, moving her head only slightly and sniffing when rain spatters up.

Above the farm, Sour Milk Gill has swollen and spilled out across the hanging valley of Gillercombe. What was a thin thread of water is now a white sheet that hangs down the side of the fell. The pass itself is covered with standing water that I kick through like a child. The rain is still falling, but the urgency has gone now. There is more space between the drops; the pressure is easing. I know that this is a transition that I probably wouldn't have noticed if I was inside. It is a change that makes me want to fill my lungs and makes me sad my family isn't here to move through this air, to be touched by this rain, to hear that sound of water on rock and tree and skin. I will think about this feeling later on as I'm driving back home. Through the rain-slicked passes of the Lakes, across the hard spine of the Pennines and down motorways that hide the landscape behind treeless embankments and service stations. The rain grows in me like the black lines that shoot across the screen of my waterlogged phone. For days after this trip, every time I get in the car the memory of this experience of rain will hit me again. The dampness will linger like a weather ghost. A mist on the windscreen. The smell of old rain on the seats. Until I finally find a sodden hat that slipped under a seat.

RAIN SWIMMING. A MEETING OF FRONTS.
Suffolk, October

From the car park, the world is divided into neat bands. The first layer is nearest – a blue metal fence, no more than knee high, and then a steep, vivid green grass bank that is scorched yellow by dog piss and barbecues. Next, a line of beach huts, two levels of them; their lapwood backs are painted in ice-cream shades of mint, blueberry, lemon, chocolate chip and strawberry. Then there is the sea. The North Sea. A cold clay sea. A cement and sand sea, waiting to be mixed.

Further down the coast, where the road is on the same level as the shore, we had watched the waves tumble hard against the massed black rocks of the sea defences, throwing themselves at the groynes. But here, with no shore visible, the surface appears only lightly creased, the waves like dark grains in wood.

There is just one final layer. One that presses down on all the others, keeping everything in place. A sky that is uniform in colour, an overwashed white tarnishing to a dishrag grey. A low, scratchy blanket of nimbostratus that stretches from Old Felixstowe to Cobbolds Point. And joining all these layers together is rain. It comes first in wide-spaced, sputtering drops, before turning to an insistent, nagging drizzle that sneaks under waterproofs and beads the rims of our woolly hats.

The dog, bored after forty-five minutes in the car, heads to the beach first, hurtling on her short Jack Russell legs down the rain-slicked concrete steps, past the beach huts, past the sea wall on the empty promenade – a concrete wave breaking back at the sea – down the four steps onto a largely shingle beach. Only on the tide line is there sand, where the tongue of the waves has licked a clean crescent in each groyne-divided section. By the time my wife, daughter and I reach the bottom, the dog, Lyra, has forgotten her urgency and is rooting around in the seaweed, moving wrack aside with her snout, marking feathers and scent points, hunting for the ripe-smelling, gull-emptied shells of shore crabs to roll in. She stops, looks at us, and pointedly shakes off the rain from the course guard-hairs on her coat.

When we lived in Brighton, the sea was ever present in our lives. And while we walked there, ate there, drank there and swam there all of the year, it was autumn and winter that we loved. When the rain sliced cheeks; when the wind howled in the shells of our ears and into the Arches of the seafront; when the sea, urged on by the weather, pushed back against the city, spitting shingle over the arsenic-green railings. Perhaps that is part of the reason why we came today. It has been fifteen years since we got married in Brighton and more than eleven since we left; moving first to the arable countryside of south Suffolk, before being washed up – through work and convenience – in Bury St Edmunds. Maybe we wanted to relive those days, to suck up the weather's energy for our own, to share a simple joy with our daughter.

But I also want to swim again in the rain. I want the double dose of negative ions to recharge. To be ready to go again at work until Christmas. It also seems a neat way of completing the circle too. I had watched the rain arrive on the west coast – rising from the Atlantic to fall in fistfuls on Seathwaite – and now I wanted to see a different band of rain finish its British visit, spluttering to a drizzly finish over the Anglian coast.

I get changed on the beach, stuffing my clothes into a carrier bag, and making sure my towel is in easy reach. A couple, walking with hoods of raincoats up, stop as their labrador investigates Lyra. The other dog bows down low and sprints off with a clatter of stones, looking over her shoulder to see if Lyra will follow. She will not. The rest of the promenade is empty. Grey with rain. The fronts of the beach huts snapped shut, pinched closed with padlocks. Further down, where the Deben swings into the sea, there are a few people fishing.

Everyone has their own way of getting into water: the slow waders, letting their body acclimatise with each step; the divers who plunge in headfirst. Mine is one of steady speed. I take off my towel robe and try not to hunch my shoulders against the rain. It has been only weeks since my soaking in the Lake District, and most of this autumn has been unseasonably warm, but today there is a bite in the rain as it hits my bare back, neck, arms and legs. The nerve endings send mixed messages to my brain, telling me that the cold has the burn of heat. I've been trying to retrain my mind, to welcome the weather in all its forms, but the body takes time to catch up.

I walk fast into the water and launch into breaststroke. The sea is surprisingly mild; it contrasts with the almost icy rain that continues to hit my face and back. In fact, out of the wind I feel warmer submerged than I had on land. I swim out towards one of the posts, topped with a metal triangle that marks the end of the groyne for boats and beach users. The swell is large enough for me to raise myself up over it, but there is no crash or spume. The sea is like a muscle, flexing, or swallowing. I feel I am being swilled. The shingle beach shelves deeply and when I turn to wave at Jen and Eliza on the beach, I can no longer touch the bottom. I love that feeling, that dropping away. The sudden lightness of body, the slight giddiness of it. I can't hear what they are shouting. Don't go too far? Is it cold?

I swim so I'm level with the end of the groynes and then turn over on to my back, feeling the chill of the sea as it reaches the back of my head and slips into my ears, while the rain falls lightly on my face. The rhythm of it feels syncopated when combined with the motion of the waves. I keep staring up, trying not to blink as the rain falls vertically. Rain this size falls as spheres not tears. The surface tension forces the molecules into the smallest shape to give the lowest surface area to volume. Larger drops, those breathless, heavy storms, flatten at the ends, becoming burger buns.

The tide is on its way in and I can feel the current trying to pull me towards the shore. The clouds look to be changing. They have been uniformly grey, a solid nimbostratus, low and rain-bearing – a cloud that stretches for miles and miles and signals a prolonged wetting. But now textures are appearing. Above me are twin bands of altostratus, forming thick dark ropes, reaching out to where the horizon has grown darker. To the right, just above the end of the pier, is a peachy streak where the sun is trying to break through. The altostratus suggests the clouds are growing and getting lower, but the direction of travel means there could be a break in the rain. The sky, like the sea, can be read and translated, just as long as you are prepared to immerse yourself.

I am getting cold. Even with my gloves on I can feel that my Raynaud's* is kicking in and the blood is draining from my fingers. I flap them in the air and Eliza misunderstands and waves back, laughing. I turn onto my front and swim over three waves, raising my chest to meet the rounded hump of them. I have seawater in my mouth, the salt on the tip of my tongue and the back of my throat. I swim

---

* A condition where the body overreacts to temperature or stress causing a feeling of cold and numbness in the hands and feet.

back towards shore and keep kicking until I feel the shingle brushing my hands. I stand, stagger forward as the waves hit the backs of my legs. Out of the water, I can feel the rain again, blowing against my back. Little spikes of cold. Eliza and Jen, bundled up in big coats, their damp hair blowing against faces that are full of cold and laughter. They are bending down to Lyra, who is standing between them with her paws on Jen's legs. They are drying her. Rubbing her wet little belly with something that looks suspiciously like my swimming towel. They laugh harder, swaddling her in it until there is just the tip of a black nose sticking out the end. Jen stands and holds her hood forward to stop the rain. She grins an apology she doesn't mean: 'She's cold, poor thing. She was crying.' The dog licks her chops. Grumbles like shingle.

We stop in a cafe to eat and warm our hands on tea that comes in fat white, porcelain pots designed to be cupped by hands. There is a large picture of Elvis, 'Goodbye Blackberry Way' playing on the radio and chips cooked in beef dripping. Lyra sighs under the table, her head resting on her paws, dark eyes looking up. My fingers are still bloodless. I wiggle them at Eliza, who grasps them in her warm hand. She says they are waxy. Like a corpse. I tell her they remind me of the kelp stalks that wash up on beaches after storms. Or the inside of crabs that chefs pull out. Dead man's fingers.

Our table is on the lowest floor, where dogs are allowed, and rather than looking down on the street, we are looking up. The rain on the window blisters the view of the seafront: an occasional pair of legs moving quickly in the rain, the dark turrets that mark the entrance to the pier, the kiosk selling ice cream, the black-headed gull blown backwards.

The English coast seems a natural place for rain. A meeting of fronts. It was a Norwegian meteorologist, Vilhelm Bjerknes, who first came up with the idea of weather fronts and borrowed the language of the First World War to describe the flare-ups of weather along the zone where warm air meets cold. Places where cold battled heat, creating barrages of rain clouds. In 1924 Tor Bergeron, who like Bjerknes was a Bergen School meteorologist, added images to the fronts. Cold fronts became a taut bunting of triangles, their shapes representing the chill of icicles, while the movement of the warm front was marked with semi-circles that symbolised the heat of a rising sun. The discovery was vital for forecasting: a working model of how a mid-latitude cyclone (where air masses meet and rise) progresses through the stages of birth, growth and decay. But it was also an entrenching of our attitudes to weather into scientific principles, into everyday language. Weather is conflict. Weather is something we battle against.

We leave the cafe and walk to the pier where music and electronic noises crunch and clonk into the rain. Eliza, holding two £1 coins, heads inside while Jen and I take Lyra for a last walk along the beach. The wind is getting up and the waves are knocking hard against the legs of the pier.

Spindrift and spray rise with juvenile gulls that wear the same sloppy brown as the sea. Far out, near the horizon, is a cargo ship rammed full of containers heading for the port. The clouds are now leaking a whisky-and-water light from above the pier. The tide is slack. In an hour or two it will go out. It will follow the rain that is heading out over the North Sea, to a different parish of weather. To the Thames, to German Bight, where water will meet water. Fresh to salt. We walk back the way we came. My hand is numb but I can feel the pressure of Jen's own hand, the tightness of her fingers between my own. I always feel as if I'm glowing after a swim and the shift of the rain, the change in the light adds to it. Makes me want to breathe more deeply. The sea, the dampness of the concrete walkway, hot oil and vinegar. As we get closer to the pier, there are still people sitting in their cars. Dug in. Drinking coffee in takeaway cups, peering through holes that have been wiped in misted windows.

HAILSTONES. KILLER RAIN.
Suffolk, October

There is a darkening to the sky. I hadn't noticed until I find myself repositioning the lamp and checking the kitchen clock. Then comes the thunder. The dog, curled up on an armchair with her nose covered by the whip of her tail, lifts her head, then lowers it with a deep sigh. The weather will break again. The unseasonably warm autumn, caused by persistent low pressure in the Atlantic and higher pressure across central and southern Europe, has fed mild air from the south/south-west for prolonged periods of October. France, Switzerland, Slovenia, Austria have all registered their warmest-ever October. Germany and Belgium have recorded their joint warmest. The UK has been frost-free. The seventh mildest autumn since records began in 1884.

In recent days my own internal weather has been off kilter too. A deep low. Poor to very poor. Perhaps the thunder is a sign that is to change too. I can lay the blame on atmospheric interference, the overloading of positive ions that comes before a storm that some have claimed causes irritability, depression, an increase in stress.[10]

There's a second rumble. Deeper, like driving too fast over a cattle grid. Wheelie bins over stones. Then it starts. Hail. Gobstoppers of ice zing off the windowpanes, shout into the shingle of the front garden and the side return. Out the front, the road is bouncing. Burning white with cold. I plod downstairs as the cat smashes through the cat flap, cold and furious. He arches, bristles. Rubs wet against my leg, his chin pressing hard against shin. I can see through the window that the hailstones are building up in the lee of the garden wall.

Jen comes downstairs and joins me at the window; asks me if I'm going out. I am tempted, but there is too much to do. The marking is piling up. Plus, by the time I get my boots and coat on, I'll probably have missed the show.

Instead, I open the back door and the windows as far as they will go and just sit and watch it hammering down, ricocheting off watering cans, fence posts, buckets and gutters. The air feels supercooled. Around the door, the ice jams together into thin white mats. One or two bounce inside, clatter like knucklebones. We pick them up, feeling the strange heat of them in our fingers. I think of the jar of silverskin onions we used to get each Christmas for my grandma. How she'd fish them out with a gadget that looked like a tiny arcade claw. I can still taste them. The crisp sharpness, the vinegar that sat fierce at the back of the throat. I pop a hailstone in my mouth and crunch it between my back teeth, thinking about how it has grown. How each skin of ice, each layer – some transparent, some hazed with air bubbles – had formed in the top of cumulonimbus thunderclouds. I breathe out, blow the cold from my tongue.

Even in mild weather, even in summer, it can be cold enough for hail. The temperature falls by 10°C for every kilometre you travel above Earth's surface. Hail forms in a cloud that is somewhere between 3 and 10 kilometres above ground. At the top of the cloud, the temperature could be –59°C or –60°C. It is here that ice particles develop from supercooled water, the particles falling towards the bottom of the cloud only to be forced back up by powerful updraughts of air within the cloud. The process is repeated and repeated until the hailstone is finally too heavy to be held.

As much as I want to get out and experience every variety in the weather I can, hail is a difficult one to enjoy. Rain might sometimes feel like needles, but it's just water after all. Hail is ice. Most of the time it's still small and harmless, but the chunks don't have to get very big to start to feel painful. I remember, aged maybe ten or eleven, being caught in a hailstorm while playing football. The game continued for a few seconds before both teams and spectators ran for cover, hands over faces or shielding backs of necks from ice that fell at speeds of 40 mph.

In 1986, the Tornado and Storm Research Organisation (TORRO) developed an internationally recognised Hailstorm Intensity Scale, with which they have classified around 2,500 storms that have been documented across the British Isles. The most intense was found to have taken place on 15 May 1697 and reached H8 on a scale that extends from H0 to H10. Reports at Offley, near Hitchin, describe hailstones as large as 445 millimetres, with 'some oval, some round, some flat'. The storm was a killer, taking the life of a shepherd. Tiles and windows were shattered. The ground was gashed and torn; great oaks were split. Another storm, on 9 August 1843, destroyed swathes of tiles in Oxford, smashed glass in the colleges of Cambridge and devastated crops across Norfolk. Officially, the biggest hailstone recorded in Britain fell on Horsham, Sussex, on 5 September 1958 and weighed 190 grams. It was produced by the H7 storm that travelled 150 kilometres from the coast of West

Wittering to Maldon in Essex. But it is likely there have been heavier, unweighed stones, with accounts from the Somerset storm of 1808 reporting lumps of ice as heavy as 220 grams.

You don't have to look back quite so far to find hail-storms that have caused damage in the UK. On 21 July 2021 hailstones, described as big as golf balls, smashed car windscreens and damaged homes in Leicestershire. Residents told the BBC that their cars had been dented and that the speed of the downpour was 'terrifying'. What's more, the impacts of climate change mean that hailstorms are more likely and that hailstones are set to get bigger and bigger – and appear in places we might not expect. In the past three years, Texas, Colorado and Alabama have seen the record broken for the largest hailstone, with stones reaching sizes of 16 centimetres across. In 2020, Libya's capital, Tripoli, was struck with even bigger hailstones, measuring as much as 18 centimetres. As climate change alters the temperature of Earth's atmosphere, it also changes the amount of moisture in the air as warmer air can hold more vapour. Modelling by researchers in the US suggests that when hail does fall, it is likely to be larger. Capable of more damage. They are unweder; they are big alien things. Egg-shaped, lumpen. Like something that has been removed from a body. Cells and tissue that have been unnaturally jammed together. Something of bone, beak and hair rather than cloud-formed.

The dog has unwound herself from her chair. Stretched and clicked over to the kitchen door where she sniffs at the air. She cocks her head to see what I'm eating and puts a cautious nose towards other hailstones that have bounced onto the kitchen tiles. They seem smaller now. The flow of them is slowing. There is the ticking on the roof of rain, but the drumming is gone. The dog sneezes. I'm not sure if it's a proper sneeze or an exaggerated signal of displeasure. She clicks back to the chair. An hour or so later, I walk to meet the kids from school. At the end of the road the last of the field maple leaves have fallen. They lie in puddles, like washed salad. Brick red on dirty water. The light is pure autumn: fat with gold. The few rags of cumulus in the sky have a nectarine blush from the low sun. But there is something new in the air too. The thin reed of winter. The temperature fell with the hail and has remained low. I felt it after I crushed that ball of ice between my teeth. I felt the breath of it.

There will be more rain to come this year – of course there will – and I find myself looking forward to it in a way I haven't felt before when contemplating the onset of winter. From here on out, showers will no longer be the providers of relief from sultry days. The droplets that fall in the coming months will land with an icy shock. But I know that I will still want to seek rain out. I've seen the sense of drama and beauty it can bring to the landscape. I've felt the thrill in the air of the storm about to break. But it's more than that, too. Walking in the rain has somehow made me more aware of my own existence. I became conscious of my thoughts and my movements through the world, how they were unique to those moments. To that time, that place, that weather. Yes, we might be left a bit soggy, a trifle damp around the edges, but the life-giving properties of water go far beyond being something to drink. Rain can nourish the soul.

That evening I look at the weather charts while lying in bed, tracking the fronts. There is sleet coming into the north. A prediction for snow on the peaks. Gale-force winds. The planet is turning and so is the weather.

FOG

If rain has associations with misery, then mist and fog is confusion. We have brain fog; we don't have the foggiest; we lose things in the mists of time. Fog is a shroud that confounds our senses, a sign of the thinning veil between worlds that leaves us fearful. But I am less concerned about what it hides, more where it hides.

I've paid little attention to fog in my life. When it's appeared, I've flicked on the fog lights, or closed the curtains against its flat grey face. I've never sought it out before. Now I'm excited at the prospect of experiencing it in all its different degrees, from the lightest mist to the densest murk; to watch the interplay of light with water droplets suspended in the air; to walk in a bubble of reduced visibility through a landscape transformed. And there is a spark of childish joy at the thought that for a couple of hours I might lose myself in a different world without the foggiest idea where I am.

MIST. RADIATION FOG. FIRST LIGHT.
Suffolk, October

I see dark shapes running on the brow of a hill. Deer, I say. My son follows the tilt of my head as I drive. The brash sweep of the headlights. Hares, he replies. He's right. There are three of them, moving in long, galloping strides without their feet ever seeming to touch the ground. A second later, maybe two, and then they are gone. Eaten up by the dark, ensnared in the nets of mist that are slung like thin white sheets across fields and hedgerows. It is the morning of my son's fourteenth birthday and the hares feel like an omen. A blessing. A touch of magic.

For the past month I have been tracking fog with little success. Fog, it seems, is hard to pin down. When I contact the Met Office for tips, I can pretty much hear them suck their teeth; they look shifty and talk about fog points and difficulties. It's a 'terribly hard to get the parts' kind of response. There are so many variables, you see, when it comes to fog.

Fog is essentially a very low-lying cloud. For clouds to form, the air must be cooled to the point where invisible moisture condenses into visible cloud. Clouds usually form as air cools while it rises, but for fog to form, the air must cool close to the ground, something that is dependent on the time of year, the time of day, cloud cover, strength of wind and the topography.

And what do you mean by fog anyway? Radiation fog,

which forms overnight as the heat from the day rises from the ground? Valley fog, where cold dense air settles and condenses in the lower parts of valleys? Advection fog when warm air passes over cold ground, like moist tropical air over snow? Upslope fog, when wind blows air up a hill (known as orographic uplift) and the air cools as it rises? Maybe evaporation fog, when cold air passes over a warm surface?

The most common type of inland fog during late autumn and winter is radiation fog. And in the flatlands of Suffolk, it is certainly the most likely. It is a fog that depends on clear skies, light winds and plenty of moisture. If there is high moisture content in the air, the temperature doesn't have as far to fall to reach the fog point. This is the reason that fog is often found lurking around rivers, lakes and seas. But this is to oversimplify the recipe. Winds are important too. They need to be gentle enough to keep the moisture in the air at the right concentration. Too strong and the moisture will be mixed too thoroughly through the air and the temperatures will be too high. Not enough wind and the moisture will settle as dew.

Fog is awkward and miraculous. Elusive. A weather of half-light and early morning that disappears with the rising temperature and the climbing sun.

Last night I had thought of the fog as I read Seth a bedtime story. It is a tradition in our house to have a story on a birthday eve. The children are autumn and winter babies, emerging into the world when it was leaning away from the sun. It seems a natural time for storytelling. Curled up together, we had read a ghost story – *The Ash-tree*, an M. R. James classic. It is a story of a curse, a witch and something dark and loathsome that emerges from the belly of the rotten tree to scuttle through the windows of a fog-dampened house. After I finished, I told him that in the morning I was heading to Great Livermere, the village where James once lived, to look for fog. The weather forecast looked promising. High pressure. Clear skies. A dipping temperature. The meres, coated in ducks and gulls, lend a dampness, a perpetual dankness to the air that sits heavy on the chest – the kids call this place Spooky Lakes. He had said he wanted to come.

It is still dark when we park up by the church and walk through white metal gates to reach the graveyard and the mere beyond. I can already see that there is a shroud of mist hanging over the water, sprung like dew blossom from the sodden grass. I take the torch and show Seth the grave of Mothersole – not really the witch from *The Ash-tree* but some long-dead and otherwise forgotten resident of Livermere whose name M. R. James borrowed. Seth takes the torch and puts it under his chin. Gurns. The light forms a semi-circle up to his nose. Highlights his cheeks and above his eyes. The rest of his face is dark and shaded by the shadow of his hood.

We go through the second gate onto the mere and behind the thick shadow of the church we can see the horizon is beginning to lighten in the east. A thin, terracotta band that fades into a milk-soaked blue. Below that, half the height of the beech and the telegraph poles, snagging on the top reaches of the scrub, is a wraith-like band of mist.

Mist and fog are essentially the same creature, both created by the suspension of water droplets in the air, causing 'obscurity in the surface layers of the atmosphere' – although they feel very different. By international agreement (which is particularly relevant for aviation) fog is the name given when the 'resulting visibility less than 1 km'.[1] Mist is less dense.

We walk forward slowly in a clot of white light cast by the torch, listening to the sound of the waking roost: shouts of gulls, glugging laughs of ducks. Above us the early birds are already on the wing, leaving in a loose stream that is a good ten metres wide.

We start to disappear into bands of mist that slice our bodies into sections. It reminds me of conjurors sawing up their smiling assistants in boxes, opening a compartment to reveal a torso where the head should be, the legs in place of a chest. Perhaps we'll emerge from the mist altered in some way too. Jumbled up. We try to take pictures with just our heads visible above the swathes of mist, but the cameras can't capture it, won't be fooled the way our eyes are. On the phones, everything looks darker, more sinister.

Sometimes, it is hard to tell if we are truly in the mist or still walking towards it. But gradually it is thickening around us. The real giveaway is the temperature, which can drop by what feels like four or five degrees when we hit a patch of proper fog. In the space of a footstep our chests tighten with cold.

Visually, fog can be quite confusing. Distances don't seem to make much sense. Research has suggested fog can convince motorists they are going more slowly than they are. As a result, they speed up, whizzing faster into the whiteness.[2] Sight becomes woolly and even sound doesn't behave in the way you would expect. The fog doesn't block sound but it does dampen it, like a pillow in a drum. The density of the water molecules changes the vibrations. Higher frequencies are particularly affected, which is why foghorns tended to use low frequencies.

As we walk, we act out, trying to make each other jump. We charge at each other from the darkness. Make sudden noises and actions to see if the other flinches. We laugh and holler and try not to notice that the noise sounds strange, the vibrations hitting the muffler of the mist. I know we are playing, but part of me wonders if this is also a ruse to prevent our surroundings from unsettling us for real. If we make each other jump, then nothing else can.

There is something about mist and fog that makes the world seem slightly unreal, insubstantial. As if the wispy nature of it has altered everything it's touched, diminishing its solidity. Perhaps that's why fog has been used as a symbol of confusion, of the supernatural. It is supposed to be the light of thin places, representing the veil between physical and eternal. It's possible to imagine anything lurking in the ethereal barrier that's hidden the rest of the world from you; that has reduced your existence to a small circle around you, into which anything could emerge suddenly, unexpectedly, without warning.

Our breath mists. We turn to clouds ourselves. It feels as though part of me is drifting off. It reminds me that we are all made from fizzing, spitting atoms that have come together in this brief blink of time after 5 billion years of being, well, something else, and soon they will zoom off again. To become gases, to be aerosols, to be clouds and rain and mud and trees. I sigh and watch my breath rise up again. Atoms already drifting on.

A sudden shout startles me back to reality, my heart racing as Seth jumps out on the path, his back hunched over like one of James's creatures. I laugh and shake my head. Call him a buffoon. He is laughing too, saying, you definitely jumped that time, I definitely got you. He acts out the horror on my face, imitates a high-pitched scream, then links his arm in mine and squeezes into me. He feels slight. Light-boned. All full of spring and energy.

The mere, when we reach it, is perfectly still and the colour of gunmetal. The path slips down to a horseshoe-shaped beach. In the low light, the mud is bright with white feathers. With flashes of shit. This is one of Lyra's favourite places to go for a walk. She bolts off and comes back with her shoulders and throat decorated with a ducky-goosey stink that Jen describes as 'boggin'. A smell that lingers in the car for days. The ducks that are closest to the water's edge are clamouring hard to get away. They half swim and half run across the water, popping out of existence when they hit the mist as if they have just hit warp drive.

There is a brick bridge that leads across the water. Low arches over black water. To take it means a longer walk, up towards the stubble fields and the pig farms. We turn left instead, the path curving back round towards the village. The light is coming. We can see the birds leaving the roost as well as hear them. The sky is a dark indigo at the top, fading to a bright white where the silhouettes of the trees mask the horizon. The gaps in the branches are like open windows. Below that, now floating at head height, is a thin layer of mist. It sits across the mere like a giant web. Lighter than silk.

Seth is excited now. He knows we're going home to a fuss. To presents and cards. To cake for breakfast. He is running in and out of the mist. His shoes and trousers are soaked. His hood is up and he's pretending to be a creature again. It's more effective in this low light; with eyes that are split between night vision and day, the shrubs assume similar shapes – all humped backs and bony haunches. The mist, an animated sheet that has been summoned by a blown whistle. I stand and watch him and laugh.

We stop once on the drive home to look back at

Livermere. The village had become a shallow cup for mist, a saucer of blue smoke. We crane our necks to look at it, turn the radio down, and open the window. The sun is climbing higher. Soon the mist will burn off and will disappear completely. I rest my hand on Seth's knee. I thank him for coming, say happy birthday. He squeezes my hand back in reply. I start to move the car, then slam on the brakes as a hare runs by, so close it almost grazes the bumper. The body is lit for a second in the fog lights I have not yet turned off; impossibly long and golden, stretched into a run as if it were dancing around the top of a Christmas card.

MISTING BREATH. FOG BREATHERS.
Newmarket, November

The lights of the town are watery in the distance. As if they were blinking up from beneath the surface of a lake. Behind me the line of trees that marks the brow of the hill disappears and reappears as the fog moves across it. The view is granular. Not quite focused. I lean against the warmth of the car's bonnet and wait. The temperature feels lower today and I can see my breath. There's something fascinating about misting breath. A visible interplay between self and world. Breathing is a fundamental yet invisible part of being alive – but here it is made visible, a physical sign that we are in the world. Our breath, our life, is suddenly written in the air.

As I walked to school when I was a child, my friends and I would pretend to smoke in cold weather. Fingers held in a V sign in front of our lips, eyes narrowed as we dragged at nothing and blew out clouds of 'smoke'. My own kids did it too when they were really young. Lord knows who they'd seen smoking. My daughter aged about three would stand with a lolly stick clamped between her teeth. She called it her 'smoker'. I smile at the memory of her sing-song voice made unnaturally gruff. Like one of those poltergeist possessions from the 1960s and 1970s.

I check my watch again: 5.55 a.m. It's nearly time now. I have been awake since half past three when I got up to take Seth to school. He was going on a trip, a two-day tour of Belgium to visit the old fronts of the First World War. To see a topography created not by freeze, thaw and flow, but by bomb, mine and man. To see something really worth avoiding.

The fog had been thick as smoke when we arrived and there was a muffled hush around the car park that might have been the weather or maybe just the time. The children were groggy, communicating in nods and shrugs, while the parents dealt in thin-lipped smiles. I stood and watched the swirl of moisture in the headlights as the coach was loaded. Most of the adults tried not to speak. Probably thinking, *If we can just do this without engaging our brains too much, we might still be able to sleep*. But I wasn't going back to bed. Not in this weather. A few of us waited to raise our hands at our children as the coach moved off. The windows were tinted though, and the fog deepened the darkness. He might have seen me; he probably didn't.

I didn't really know where I was going. I started off heading towards the Fens, where last night the fog had already been reaching out its tendrils, tracking the ghosts of rivers by the railtracks, settling into dips of the A14 like spoonfuls of milk. But I turned off early, following the backroads past the locked gates of stables and the high, blocky hedges of training tracks and gallops. I parked halfway up Warren Hill, looking down towards the town of Newmarket. The hill itself is part of the Newmarket Ridge. It is a grand name, evoking images of thin escarpments of rock. Crags. Snow-tipped peaks. But this hill is gentle to the point of disappearing. A 'low topographic prominence'. The ridge, also known as the East Anglian Ridge, is a line of small chalk hills that curves like a spine for 60 kilometres, from near Bishop's Stortford in Hertfordshire, through Cambridge and peters out near Sudbury. The hills themselves give a rare bit of a roll to the countryside. Although their sides may occasionally steepen, the peaks themselves are flat.

Newmarket is home to around 3,000 racehorses, about one for every six humans in the town. The Warren Hill canters – which rise by more than 40 metres over the last half kilometre – are visited by about 16,000 horses each month, with the busiest time being early in the morning.

I can see a string of lights now, coming down the hill. Three or four white lights and two green. They swing like lanterns, but they are held at an improbable height. The horses emerge from the fog as formless silhouettes, their shapes turned to blocks, dark against the skyline. Occasionally I can see the peak of a rider, or a disembodied headtorch that swings to the rhythm of the horse's hips. The light smudges the air; the fog glints.

I can hear snatches of conversation. Hard, flinty words against the softness of the fog and the fluid nature of their own rolling movements. There's talk of someone's house, *a right shithole. Should have seen him. Right prick. Yeah, mate. One to avoid.* They move slowly past me, eight of them, heading now towards the bottom of the hill, where the jockey will move his left hand, pulling the reins tight and swinging the horse round to face the start of the gallops. There will be a pause, perhaps, a kick and then he will rise above the movement of the horse's back, keeping his body over the ridge of the horse's withers. He will crouch. Keep his back long, his eyes forward, elbows close to the knees, propelling his body forward with the horse, climbing the hill with him, his heartbeat rising as he watches the trees appear black and low from the fog between the horse's ears.

A minute passes in silence after they're out of sight and then another. There is the sound of a low, corvidy rasp. Magpie? Jackdaw? No. A horse breathing. The sound of 55-litre lungs filling and emptying, moving oxygen to blood and muscle. Three lights are moving up the hill fast. I don't know if it is the fog or the artificial Polytrack surface the horses are running on, but strangely I can't hear their hoofbeats. The paradiddling bass of ground being covered. The movements are disconcertingly smooth in the fog, the shadows gliding up the hill, with only the snatched breaths evidence of the speed and the effort. The shape of them emerges for a second. The dark form of a rider crouched over a horse's neck and then the fog swallows them again.

I wonder what the horse thinks. Being pointed and run towards an unseen target. Moving through something that appears solid in the beam of the jockey's headtorch. I wonder if the conditions help the jockeys. With the world boiled down to a matter of metres seen from between the horse's ears, can they focus more on the breathing, on feeling the mechanics of muscle, tendon and bone? Later I will watch a video with a racehorse trainer, talking about these gallops. He will refer to how they are looking to see if the horse is 'as normal'. He describes the breathing as listening to their wind. I like the idea of a horse possessing some elemental force. That a galloping horse becomes more flesh, blood, sinew and sweat. The horse is a wind maker. A fog breather.

There is a breeze and as dawn whitens the sky, the fog follows the horses up the hill. I think it is the fog lifting rather than the forming of hill fog (when wind blows air up a

hill, which cools as it rises, allowing moisture to condense*).
At the bottom of the hill the town has clicked into focus. I
can see the twin tracks of the white barriers that marshal
the two gallops, the long white building with black windows where the horse boxes are parked, the red-brick wall
of Heath House stables. But up the hill there is still cloud.
I walk to the edge of it and watch as the horses emerge,
bringing with them their own fog. The mist of breath from
flared nostrils, the sweat that emerges from the rugs on their
backs. They shake their heads, snorting, as if to clear them
of this strange stuff that extends blinkers, that fills their
mouths like rags. Further up the hill, three rooks sit on a
line on the white barrier. Neat, black, folded shapes against
a swirl of fog that looks greyer now as the day brightens.

The fog is definitely shrinking. From the top down, from
the outside in. Fizzing away like a pill in water to leave a
powdery blue in the upper reaches the colour of a starling's
egg. Fog, with its moisture, its dripping nature, is often seen
as a sign of 'poor' weather. But it can forecast the opposite.
A summer fog is for fair weather. A winter fog will freeze
a dog.

The rooks move as more horses come past them, walking
downhill, their jockeys swaying. The birds hop past each
other, taking it in turns to be the furthest bird along, before
they fly off, up into the light.

* A process called orographic uplift.

SMOG. TIMELESSNESS. GHOST RIVER.
Wicken, November

The sign at the entrance says 'Welcome to Wicken Fen, loved for the biggest skies and the tiniest creatures'. Today the sky has grown so big the land has disappeared. The clouds have lowered, erupted from the ground where they were sleeping. On the drive here, along main roads where morning traffic hiccoughs nervously along, bumper to bumper, visibility was down to something like 200 metres. Away from the main road, the rear lights of the car in front, bright as a sucked cigarette, are the only marker for where the road goes.

This fog has come as something of a relief. The weather over the past two weeks has been strangely mild, creeping up to 19°C. Even at night the thermometer has hovered in the high teens, refusing to sink, refusing to respond to Earth's slow tilt away from the sun. It's comforting to have this return to seasonality.

It is early and the fen is still empty. The visitor centre and cafe, larch lapped and tar black, are closed. Behind them is the last surviving wooden wind pump in the Fens. Its white sails are barely visible. Noticeable for the change in texture in the air rather than a change of colour. I carry on walking, keeping the pump and the thin, straight dyke of Wicken Lode to my right. The world is smaller, shrunk down to my immediate surroundings. It is green grass and the burnt yellow of fallen willow leaves. It is the faint smudge of trees and dense banks of reeds, their heads bent and loaded with water. I find that I walk the same way I did in the rain: squinting, trying to make things out. It feels good to be out of the car. I kept turning the wipers on in an attempt to clear the view, the same way I sometimes turn the dial of a silent radio down when I'm concentrating.

Lyra is less keen about being out. She is a fair-weather dog: spooked by wind, loathes getting wet, can't stand the cold. It turns out she is not best pleased with fog either. I think she feels the same way most humans do – kicking back against the changes to the senses, the new lens that has been slotted into place. Perhaps it's time she changed her outlook too. A few biscuits certainly help.

I stop under a pollarded willow, its branches lode-straight, and listen to the sound of water falling. The fog condenses and falls to create the smallest, most gentle tapping on leaves, like the knocking of a beetle inside wood. Lyra exhales sharply through her nose. The way she does when she is really annoyed by something: the cat being where he shouldn't, someone moving while she is sleeping on their lap. Across the lode is another wind pump. The frame has been rubbed out by the fog, so the metal sails appear to hang on nothing, as if they are hovering; held in place only by the thickness of the air.

It is a thickness that has long been viewed with suspicion. While rain might be associated with sadness, fog was considered much more dangerous – something that can impact both mind and body. In the sixteenth century, the Dutch physician Levinus Lemnius said that in 'a thick and cloudy air, men are tetric, sad and peevish'.[3] Writing his *Anatomy of Melancholia* in the following century, Robert Burton seemed to agree. He even made maps of air to be avoided for the sake of health: the marshes of Romney, of Essex and of course the 'fen-sucked fogs' of the east. Lands that are low, water-soaked and mist-shrouded, it was believed, should not be risked. We should, Burton said, head for the hills. For those whose mood is affected by weather, the lack of sunlight in foggy conditions can be a dampener; the eeriness of a place shrouded in mist can put us on edge. But humans have created something much more sinister out of fog.

By the 1600s, the widespread use of coal fires was blackening and damaging buildings. The smoke mixed with water particles and formed impenetrable walls of fog that sat heavy on the chest. The 'fog and filthy air' of *Macbeth* would no doubt have been seen by his audience as a physical threat as much as a symbol of moral and political confusion. The diarist John Evelyn, writing in the 1670s, described London as being smothered in a 'fuliginous and filthy vapour'.[4] On some days, he said, the city is 'eclipsed with such a cloud of sulphur as the sun itself is hardly able to penetrate'. By the eighteenth and nineteenth centuries, with the centralisation of factories, the 'old-particulars' – possibly named after London Particular Madeira (a wine fortified with brandy) – had deepened. One of the worst of these fogs took place in the winter of 1813 when movement across the capital became almost impossible. The Birmingham Mail Coach took seven hours to travel to Uxbridge, while the Prince Regent was forced to give up his journey after travelling just two or three miles in as many hours. In 1873 one fog lasted seven days and the mortality rate rose to 40 per cent above average.

Dickens, writing some two decades before, presents us with a fog that has the ability to be almost everywhere. In the opening of *Bleak House* fog is moving and intentional; it is animal, plant and mineral: 'Fog on the Essex Marshes, fog on the Kentish heights. Fog creeping into the cabooses of collier-brigs, fog lying out on the yards, and hovering in the rigging of great ships; fog drooping on the gunwales of barges and small boats. Fog in the eyes and throats of ancient Greenwich pensioners, wheezing by the firesides of their wards.'[5] Like Burton, Dickens and many others also still linked the fogs with the flatlands of the east. The east wind, 'neither good for man nor beast', brought fog full of contagion to the capital and the surrounding counties.

Although the Smoke Nuisance Abatement Act was introduced in 1853, two years after *Bleak House* was written, fog continued to blend with pollution. The strangeness of fogs thickened by smoke turned the air to green-tinged peasoupers and to 'chocolate-coloured' palls that hid Londoners from each other while also concealing the horrors of Mr Hyde. In the perpetual shroud, a monster stamping on children like a squat Grendel of the industrial age, seemed entirely believable. Could it be that it was here that the fog as supernatural stage setting really came into its own? That fog, already associated with pestilence, with transforming even well-known landscapes into places that evoke the eerie through their confusion of the senses, became a horror character in its own right?

Perhaps the most famous fog in the UK took place in London in 1952. By then a new word had been coined to describe the coming together of pollution and suspended water particles: smog. Britain was a world leader in the production of coal, which continued to be the main source of fuel when it came to heating homes. The home fires, the hearth, with its almost folkloric associations, kept burning. Then in December, with fires burning against night-time temperatures of –5°C and daytime temperatures of less than zero, an area of high pressure arrived from the north-east. A blanket of warm, moist air was held over London. The cold temperatures condensed vapour to fog, and the chimney smoke and emissions, rather than drifting away, became trapped. The pollution provided nuclei for the formation of water droplets, making them tiny and in increased concentration, producing a fog that the Met Office said was 200 metres thick and had a visibility as low as 5 metres.

This fog would last for days. At Kingsway in the heart of London, 114 continuous hours of fog were recorded from 5 to 9 December, with 69 of those hours having a visibility of less than 50 metres. Navigating the streets was fraught with danger. Air traffic was suspended. Trains and boats were cancelled. There had been heavy fogs and smogs before, but this time the fog picked locks and jimmied windows. Newspaper reports suggested that audiences seated in the balcony at Festival Hall were unable to see the stage; a performance at Sadler's Wells was halted for the same reason. One poor factory worker in west London went missing for three hours after leaving the staff canteen and being swallowed by the smog.

But the impacts of the smog would outlast the weather. The *Guardian* reported at the time that surfaces, indoors and out, were left 'greasy' and covered with 'grime' while both hospitals and morgues continued to fill up. Throughout that week, hospitalisations were up by almost 50 per cent due to a surge in respiratory conditions and the government tallied that 3,000 people had died as a result of the smog. Flowers and caskets were both said to be in short supply. In reality, the consequences of the smog were even worse. In 2012, researchers from Johns Hopkins University suggested that the combination of fog and pollutants had led to 12,000 deaths, while children exposed to the smog were 20 per cent more likely to develop asthma.[6]

Thankfully this sort of smog is in the past in the UK. Even if air pollution is still an issue, air quality is much improved. The fog has returned to its natural state. Eerie but mostly not actually life-threatening.

The path bends round, past a tree that stands broken topped and barkless as if the fog had rubbed it away. On the water's edge, the fog has been captured on spider webs. They are everywhere: intricate, symmetrical Halloween webs, made from silk that is ounce-for-ounce stronger than steel. There are webs that look like cartoon-perfect hexagons; lace clothes on spiked grasses; parachutes and tents in the oak trees; messy cats cradles in the reeds; single filaments spun from a tiny body that have bound trees together, long strands stretched, taut like tightrope between bramble and hawthorn, each berry a bead of blood. At first it hadn't crossed my mind that the webs were always there and only now had become visible, now that the moisture had caught the light.

Two cormorants fly over, tracking the lode. One black, the other white-chested. I stand while the dog sniffs around the water's edge, looking at how the surface has taken on the colour of the sky. At the horizon the fog and the lode flow together. The fenland word for a man-made waterway also describes a vein of mineral. As if the water were something solid. A calcite in rock. Hard and bright as teeth.

The trail crosses Monk Lode and I think goes between Baker's Fen and the mere but there are other routes and I'm getting confused. The dog sniffs at me with frustration every time I pause. She wants to get on with it. I have a terrible sense of direction; there is a good chance of going wrong whatever the weather. I think how stupid it would be to get lost when everything is straight lines and right angles. When it is all signposted paths. I tell the dog that it's because of the fog. She puts her head on one side, her ears moving. There are more birds now. Waterfowl. Their calls sneak through the creases of the fog. The *haw-hawing* laugh of ducks, the false-teeth whistle of widgeon and that strange, throaty wobble of shovelers. Behind it all, deeper, like a rattling engine, are geese. We follow the sounds to a wire fence where a woman with shoulder-length hair and a dark woollen hat has a hand shielding her eyes. She peers into the fog as if looking at something bright and burning. She is searching for a herd of Konik ponies that graze the fen. Trying to make sure they are all right. She gestures towards Barnet's Fen, where grass and mere slide into imperceptible greyness in a little less than 200 metres. It's hard at the best of times, but in this, it's impossible, she says.

I show her my map, point at where I think I am and she traces it with a finger in reply. Forward. Then right.

Down by the farm, then right again. She re-angles the map so she can see it better. The fog has created droplets of water on her hat that look like tiny seed pearls. She suggests an alternative route and another one, and I know that I am lost again and just nod out of politeness, to make her stop. Lyra sits staring at me. Trying to judge if this will be a long conversation. The volume of the birds has increased. Perhaps something has disturbed them. There is a *whomp* of wings that sounds like the ignition of a boiler clicking on, a smudge of black movement against the blind whiteness of the fog.

I keep going in the same direction. I don't want to turn right yet. To go right would be to start to close the loop and, despite not always being sure exactly where I am, I'm enjoying being out in the fog. There's something about it that feels like the relentless march of time has slowed, or even frozen in place. Like a ghost story I read when I was in my teens, about a man who, while camping in a forest, becomes trapped in a bubble of time. He eats and sleeps but always wakes to the same place, at the same time. The pictures I found in my research of London in the smog had the same feeling. Pictures that show lamplighters tending flames, with the gas lamps doing little more than creating an ethereal glow that transforms people into dark-bodied ghosts. It seemed like a place of perpetual night. The sun turned to a dull, fog-draped moon on a dawnless day.

I wonder if it's because I'm getting older but I notice

the passage of time more these days. It seems speeded up, the people around me sprinting through life. But here time has stilled. It has been captured in the dew point. And I find that I'm relishing this sense of timelessness, the feeling that I've been released from its shackles.

I follow the path until I hit something that looks as if it might be concrete. It seems more solid than the clay and silt tracks I've been on so far. Behind me in the distance, slightly elevated on a dyke wall, is the figure of a man, cut off at the knees. A black shadow against the exhaust-fume grey of the sky. The light is milky. It reminds me of my mum pouring Dettol into the bathroom sink to deal with cuts from bikes and skateboards, the water clouding over.

Usually it is easy to navigate here. On clear days, landmarks are easy to make out in the flatness, but now I'm not quite sure. I think I'm at the edge of the reserve now as, to my left, there is farmland. The fog is not as thick here. I guess the land is drained and there is less moisture in the earth to create radiation fog. I can see over the deep, green V of the dyke to a field that has been ploughed and tilled to a peaty black crumb. I stop to get my bearings and to let Lyra sniff at something – the moisture in the air amplifies track scents. If you want to track people, living or dead, when it's foggy, snowing lightly or just after rain is best.[7] A cyclist goes past and Lyra growls until the man's luminous back, bisected with a spray of liquid mud, disappears into the fen-sucked fog.

We find the Koniks the warden was searching for clinging to the same edge of the reserve. There is snorting. A
lip-blown exhalation and the fog on my right moves. Grows
heads and feet. The ponies are the colour of a *Jekyll and Hyde*
fog. A hard grey with hints of chocolate brown. There are
loads of them. Some pull up grass noisily by the root, while
others stand, legs braced as if they are ready for the world to
roll. Two rear up against each other. Bulky. Barrel-chested,
but thinned to shadows in the fog.

These animals are hardy things. An old breed. So old
that there is a myth that the Konik is a direct descendant
of the Tarpan, supposedly wild horses that roamed across
Europe.[8] So old its name just means pony. Or maybe its
name comes from its utilitarianism. Conservation charities
use them to keep scrub down, to make sure fenland doesn't
transform. Koniks don't mind going into water, even up to
their chests if needs be. They'll knock holes into reedbeds
and help create that magical ecological buzzword – habitat
mosaics, where different habitats converge and biodiver-
sity flourishes. Why give a does-what-it-says-on-the-tin
breed a fancy name? They do look beautiful today, though.
The fog prettifies their colours, deepens their smokiness
and adds drama to their movements, just as it did to the
million pounds of horseflesh in Newmarket. Sounds that I
wouldn't have noticed before, the deep lung-filling breaths,
seem clear and give them a sense of solidity despite being
partly obscured by the mist.

Other things seem prettier too. The farmyard – with its deep, pungent puddles, its steaming muck spreader, the bales sitting on beds of plastic and tyres – is softened. An air of mystery surrounds it. I raise a hand to the tractor driver, pick up Lyra so she doesn't get completely coated in shit and walk down to where I think the bridleway leads back towards Wicken.

The fog has recovered its denseness. It's hard to see much beyond the reed heads, which seem bowed and laden with water. Above the reeds, I can just see a dark, bumpy band of land beyond. The outline of a tree with two trunks. Each empty crown forming a silhouetted lung. There is a bird hide with a view out onto the fen. On the wall are images of lapwing, teal, wigeon and short-eared owl. But out of the hatch there are no birds, no movement of any kind. A scrape or small mere the colour of lead marks the point at which reed turns to rough grass. The sky, low enough to dead-head the tallest reeds, stretches from horizon to horizon.

It is colder in the hide. My breath steams. I pick Lyra up again and put her inside my old jacket, rubbing the wet and the mud from her stomach. I carry her the rest of the way, over a bank that is raised over the Fens and connects again with the path I had used setting out. I can feel her rumbling away against my chest, the way that she does when she is either pleased with something or mildly annoyed. A low *hnnnnggggg*. Her snout is out the top of my coat. Angled up like a Goya painting. If I look down, she pokes the bottom of my chin with her cold nose. Rumbles again. Tries to lick me.

The cafe is open now but mostly empty, apart from the woman at a till and a warden with a travel mug. He asks if it was peaceful out there. Not many walkers around today. He tells me that he loves watching the fog come in over the fen. Swilling over the lodes. Swamping the Carr. The way he talks makes me think of something animal coming home to roost. Something that is at home here. And, of course, it is. Wicken is the only large area of fen that has never been drained, where the fog still forms above the water as it would have done in so much of the surrounding area before humans began to meddle.

Huge areas of landscape have been transformed by drainage, the water pumped away down new straight cuts that eventually rose above the slumping, dry peat. In the fields you can sometimes see where the water used to flow and braid. There are darker patches of earth, known as rhondons – black veins, like the inside of a prawn, that spread out across the fields.

The warden is upbeat though. There is so much to worry about environmentally, but there is good news here, he says. So much is being done to reset and restore the Fens. He talks about water being added, about re-wetting huge tracts of land.

I used to think that the fog was like a ghost river, a memory of the flowing water of the Fens transformed into a great white wisp. But perhaps it is a ghost of the Fens yet to come. A joyful, fun ghost. A glimpse of a rewetted, rewilded and transformed land.

HILL FOG. VALLEY FOG. SPECTRES.
Peak District, November

It was already dark when I got here last night; driving through a yellow warning for rain to track down fog in the Peak District. In the lights from the road and the villages I could already see a mist riming the slumped mounds of the hills. The ridges softened; furred. I had walked over the fields, trying to get a quick lie of the land, and wandered into the grit-stone prettiness of the village with its outcrops of tea rooms and plateaux of pubs. I went for a drink and listened to strangers talking about the weather, their vowels smoothed and rounded. I had lingered, head down, nursing the dregs. Not loving the thought of crawling into a bivvy bag with a tree root for a pillow.

I've been to Castleton before. Just once. That time it was all about the weather too. Of course it was; since I've started writing this book, I've been surprised by how weather frames my memories, how it is the lens through which I recall so many details of places and events. I was about six or seven then and walking with my parents and my older brother. We had been just coming into the village when a snowstorm hit. I remember the strange whiteness of the light, the feeling of snowflakes flying into my face, closing my eyes against them and feeling them kissing cold against my lowered lids. I remember the iciness in my fingers, a feeling like pins stuck so deep they lodge and quiver in bone. I don't know whether it is because the story was told so often by my parents, or because it is a genuine memory, but I remember a feeling of – I can't think of another word for it – being lifted. With the wind at our backs, the gusts had been so strong they had made a sail of me. Each forearm had been gripped by a parent as my feet lifted off the ground, my chest knocked forward, toes pointed and dragging through loose stone and mud, as though I were pretending to be an aeroplane. You would have blown clean away, they said. I remember the pain in my hands caused by the burn of the cold not being rubbed away for hours. How within the caravan, which rocked as the wind slapped into it like a belly against water, I had cried as the blood squeezed back down narrowed veins.

It is still dark when I get up in the morning. Dawn is a good hour away and my headtorch is not much help. The beam knocks against the fog, bounces back with sparks and glitter. I can remember the way from last night, when I'd walked to the pub. The 16-kilometre loop of the Great Ridge sticks to that route for at least the first couple of kilometres:

through the narrow, hip-crunching stone gate in the corner of the field; through the sheep field, across the stream and onto the lane by Peakshole Water. The gurgle hidden in the trees. I sniff. The scent of old orchards. The cheesy warmth of manure. It feels cold. Cold enough for me to want to dig my hands in my pockets, wishing my water bottle wasn't taking up all the space, that I didn't have maps and a banana in there as well. That I had brought gloves. It's really starting to feel like autumn. I had told the kids the same thing as I walked and talked on the phone with them last night. I'd heard about their afternoon, told them to be good, that I'll see them tomorrow. They had in turn told me to be careful, and had laughed when a tawny owl hooted so loudly it sounded like a cartoon.

I reach the first houses of the village. They are made from the same stone as the buildings in the centre but they have the neatness, the coolness of new-builds. There are some lights on in kitchens, while others are still soft with dark and sleep or flicker with the rippling blue light of a TV. On the walls outside, fitted like flags between windows, are early Christmas trees. Their twinkling lights dulled by the fog. It has a surreal quality, the same feeling as when you're pulled from the tail end of a dream. A sensation of silkiness that disappears no matter how hard your brain tries to hold on to its threads. On my left is the pub where I ate last night. But now I'm going straight on, towards the old part of the town that is overlooked by the remains of the Norman castle. A squat red thumb against the green of Cave Dale.

I walk more quickly now. I want to get up onto the ridge, to see if I can get above the fog. I don't know if it is possible, if the hills are high enough. But I have been hoping to see a cloud inversion; one of those times when the valleys swell with fog and you are able to walk above the clouds in bright sunlight. A cloud inversion is, in reality, a temperature inversion. In normal conditions, meteorologically speaking, the higher you go up the colder it gets (about 2°C for each 300 metres). But inversions see that flipped. A layer of cold air is trapped at ground level, pressed down by a firm hand of warm air.

Predicting inversions is tricky. When I've talked to people about it, there have been more sucked teeth. I've been directed to apps and websites that generate dew points and probabilities. So I know the conditions here have been right. There has been a period of almost stationary high pressure, allowing the gradual descent of cold air with moisture in the lower layers of the atmosphere. And I know inversions happen here. I've seen the photos. Pictures of walkers perched on boulders on top of Kinder Scout, the fog looking like the head on a beer, cut level with the top of the glass. There are images taken from Mam Tor and the Great Ridge over Edale and Hope Valley showing the valley boiling with fog, broken by a spire or the great grey stack of the cement factory.

It is to the Great Ridge I'm heading now, a spine of rock that stretches for 3 kilometres from Mam Tor at the western edge to Lose Hill and separates the vales of Edale and Castleton. From the village I start to climb up through the dry valley of Cave Dale. The walls of the valley are almost perpendicular and in places reach heights of 50 metres. Perhaps this, combined with the ruins of Peveril Castle, is what makes the whole valley seem architectural, as if this had once been a building; a fortress that the hills took back and petrified. But the depth of the valley is all due to the interactions of water and limestone. It was glacial meltwater that cut the rocks here before the water melted through the limestone and found a route underground. The caverns below Cave Dale collapsed, making the valley deeper. The limestone scooped like grapefruit. Dissolved and carried like salt. Just 200 years ago there used to be an arch over Cave Dale. But it fell. Maybe a result of rain, more likely the frost that still shatters rock and causes boulders to fall. The whole ground is littered with rocks that turn under the feet and make walking slow.

I stop and look back to where the valley is at its narrowest, where a sign says that the rocks are the remains of coral reefs. The tide has long been out, the river has long been sunk, but this place still holds the memory of moisture. A bank of fog is pushing up the hill. A thin stream of water droplets flowing uphill. Creeping with what seems to almost be intentionality. The castle has already disappeared.

The path levels out and follows a dry-stone wall. The signs say Limestone Way. But this is now open fields and the fog is deepening. At first, I can feel it in the temperature. A damp coldness. The way the light no longer seems to penetrate. Then the green of the land simply ends. It is as if a child has started a drawing and not completed the sky – no yellow circle for the sun, curved 'm's of birds, or the wrist-aching scribble of blue. And then I can see the fog blowing towards me, powdery and thick, consuming walls, draping pale and heavy over the scrub of grass. I feel a thrill at its approach, like a child waiting for a wave. I know it will wrap around me, transform my world once more. Behind me the sun gasps low and gold onto puddles, then it too is bandaged in white. Cattle appear and disappear as the visibility dips towards 100 metres, maybe less.

The fog helps focus the mind in the same way darkness does. To perceive the world in a new way, to feel a completely different realm emerging in this new thicker light. It is harder to navigate in fog than in darkness. However thick the night is, it is thinner than fog. My body strains against the fog in a way that it doesn't against the night. There is a circle of clear visibility that bubbles you. But to push beyond that, through water droplets, is impossible. The trick is not to try. Float in the fog. Focus on what you can experience, not what you cannot. I start to concentrate on the few things around me that emerge as I pass by: the perfect twists of barbed wire; the colour of the lichens on the dark stones of the wall, some yolk-coloured and dusty, others arsenic-green scabs. It is early, but I wonder if anyone else is up here. Has the fog stopped or delayed other walkers? Perhaps they are up here and I haven't realised. All walking cheerfully oblivious within a metre of each other.

The temperature has dropped. When I stop I can feel the contrast between the air and the hotness of my back. I keep following the wall, until it meets another. I cross on a stile formed by large stones and follow a new path, a farm track now, with a wire fence to the right and a wall that seems a little less straight than the previous one. I can hear the high squeaky cheep of a meadow pipit. A song that sounds as if it would be removed with a squirt of WD40. There is a curlew too. Higher. Plaintive. Moving somewhere nearby. The silence rolls back in. Flows with the fog. Wet and sticky. Fields of cattle turn to sheep, their backs marked with a highlighter blue. The fields themselves are changing too. Rucking and bucking. I can see that the fogline is no longer a straight line of grassland, but is punctuated by rocks.

There are shapes of houses. No, just one house. A farm-house with a barn. There is nothing unusual about it really, but the fog lends an eeriness to it. It makes it feel like an unexpected presence, a Brigadoon building that appears at dew point. The fog somehow sucks the solidity from it. Turns grit stone to thick air. I can hear a road now. The *shush* of it. It won't be long before I can see headlights and tail lights, fuzzy white and red pins of light in the murk.

I walk alongside the road for a hundred metres and turn right into a grove of beech trees and the car park of Mam Tor. There is a sign with an illustration showing the view from its flat top over the bowl of the Edale Valley. The drawing shows views over moor and rivers, no houses. There are a few people clustered on the top. An ancient hilltop fort, it says. The steep sides of this high hill made it the perfect stronghold – a great place to see and be seen. Unless it's foggy, of course. I'm not sure of the reason, what geographical quirk is at play, but the fog has pulled away here and returns only as I climb the steps up to the peak. There is one person walking the other way. Pulled along at speed by a retriever with a lolling tongue. He appears and disappears so quickly, there's no time to say hello. But I can hear him telling the dog off as he runs to keep up. The click of claws, the slap of feet. One of them wheezes as they go. *Bloody hell, Pongo. Bloody hell.*

The fog wraps back round the hill as I near the peak. I'm just following the flagstones and the world is nothing more than grey stone and a bright fog. The walk is not hard but I do feel more out of breath than I was expecting. Even without pollution fog can make exercise more challenging, increasing the humidity levels and decreasing the amount of oxygen. Research has shown that the low temperature of morning may also increase the chances of acute respiratory or cardiovascular diseases.

The surface levels out, the path leading to a sloping

circle of limestone capped by a summit cairn that is so neat it looks more like part of a house. I wonder if those who put this in place were thinking of eyes. The curved circle, the iris; the cairn, a vertical pupil that looks out across the valleys, hills and towns of the peaks. But today there is nothing to see, however hard you look, however large your pupil. Those little people on the sign, standing on the curved lip of Mam Tor, where the earth had slipped to form other hills, would see nothing but water droplets dancing in front of their faces.

I walk around, trying to get my bearings. East for Hope Valley, west for the Eden Valley, north-east to Losehill. I do feel a bit disappointed. I was hopeful that my predictions were good and that I would arrive to look down on fog that had washed into the valley like the sea at high tide. But there must have been a factor wrong; the temperature not quite right, or some breeze pulling slightly in the wrong direction. I'm cross with myself too at my own reaction. For demanding a certain weather, for not being more accepting of nature doing its own thing.

In any case, I have seen an inversion once before, not that I realised what it was then. I was a child, on another walking holiday with my parents and my brother. We were somewhere in North Wales, maybe Snowdonia. All I remember is that we stopped for cake – a favourite fruit cake wrapped in multiple skins of clingfilm – and as I ate I realised we were above the clouds. I didn't know about temperature inversions or clouds rising and falling. The sky was a childishly simple thing. It was blue and sometimes there were clouds that appeared at the top of it. If I was above the clouds, it could only mean that I was fantastically high. That thought had made me dizzy, had made me want to cling to the ground that bit harder. But I was also taken by the textures that I could see. The clouds had looked so different from above. It seemed that if I had slipped off and landed in that bunched-up stratus it might have held me like a blanket under a window.

But this fog, this cloud, does not look as if it would hold me. I put a hand up and push. It reminds me of the video games I play badly with my children, where it is possible to fall off the edge of the world, the character toppling forever into an unanimated abyss. I shuffle closer to the ridge edge and look down again. We think of fog as a ghostly setting, a place that is suited for hauntings. But fog creates its own ghosts too.

Brocken spectres, from the German *Brockengespenst*, also known as the spectre of the Brocken, are the magnified shadows of people that have been cast onto a cloud bank. Named for its multiple appearances in the frequently foggy but easily accessed German peak of Brocken in the Harz mountains, the spectre is formed when the sun, or other bright light, shines from behind someone who is looking down from a ridge into fog. The light projects the shadow through the suspended water droplets, with the shadow often appearing gigantic due to an optical illusion.* I've only seen pictures of them online. Strange figures whose limbs seem to have been pulled out of proportion: legs widening to trunks, while arms twizzle off to dust. They look like ink drawn on a wet page, their heads sometimes crowned by a halo of rainbow light. A *Heiligenschein*. A glory.

Coleridge captured the phenomenon in a poem at the start of the nineteenth century after a visit to Germany:

> And art thou nothing? Such thou art, as when
> The woodman winding westward up the glen
> At wintry dawn, wh're o'er the sheep-track's maze
> The viewless snow-mist weaves a glist'ning haze,
> Sees full before him, gliding without tread,
> An image with a glory round its head;
> The enamoured rustic worships its fair hues,
> Nor knows he makes the shadow, he pursues![9]

But there are no such shadows on this peak today. The sun is in the wrong place and is, of course, still swaddled in fog.

A week or so later, when the fogs rise again on my drive to the school where I teach, I will try and find my Brocken spectre again. I stop the car on the empty playground and stand in front of the headlights, which are pointed out over

---

* The observer believes their shadow on nearby clouds to be at the same distance as objects seen through any gaps in the cloud.

the fog that now glitters over the fields. The fog moves in the darkness. Reminds me of cigarette smoke under the table lights of a snooker room. I walk forward, expecting the shadow to appear any second, just as it did on those internet videos. I hold my breath. I'm braced and ready. But there is nothing. I'm still standing, limbs taut and splayed, when a colleague drives by. Then another. I decide to give up just before the school bus pulls in and anyone can find the sight of me more alarming than anything the fog could create.

I haven't gone far from the peak when I feel the light changing. The fog begins to lift, to drift off in swathes. I can see it in sheets along the spine of the ridge that is now appearing behind and in front of me. It reminds me of how paper burns on a fire. The way holes appear, and light burns through. There are patches of blue sky now, their edges still milk-soaked, but I can see the sharp edges of trees and plantations, the wobbling jog of dry walls, and beyond that in the distance the villages of Hope and Castleton. So far away that they have the same texture as that lichen on a stone. Down in the shadow of the ridge, I can see a farm. A dog is barking. The sound bounces from the stone, rises up with scraps of fog that make the light gruellish and claggy. The peak of Mam Tor has faded to shadow as more fog rises to the height of the Great Ridge, mapping the changes in temperature. It looks as if the fog is shifting and will soon spill from one valley into another. The view across to Kinder Scout is still hidden but I find I really don't mind after all. In some ways I prefer the fog. It feels somehow more honest, more engaging. It roots you to the place you are, rather than lifting you above it into something picturesque and more abstract.

I keep walking along the ridge, through the lowest point at the old coffin route at Hollins Cross, until I get to Back Tor, a rocky outcrop with an almost sheer escarpment that points down into Edale. The cliff face itself is curved, the bands of strata that form it exposed like the rings of a hailstone, like dentine in an old fossilised tooth. On top of the craggy brow stands a singular pine that is spindly black against the flat mattness of the fog. It is a scramble up to the top; the rocks move and split under my feet. By the top I stand on an anvil of rock and walk out to the edge. I consider sitting with my feet dangling into the milkiness of the fog, to relive that idea of walking on cloud. The peak is well trodden, flat and brown, and there's a man already here. He's sitting with arms wrapped around his legs, his chin resting on his knees. We say hello, but I get the feeling he doesn't want to talk, he just continues to look out over Edale. The view is starting to clear here too, but it is still like looking through smeared glass. The features are not sharp. The peaks are outlines. They don't rear or impose.

All around me I can see that stones have been piled into cairns. Some are just three stones tall, but others are much bigger: nine or ten pieces of shale, lumps of limestone, all balancing precariously. I think of how the fog had been balancing on the ridge, the peculiarity of the flatness of the cloud perched on a spike of rock.

I walk around quietly looking at the stones, wondering why they are here. Later I will look it up and see that it's just become a tradition. That people follow those who came before them. Faced with a cairn, they will create their own. A foothold, a way to shape something, to leave something of themselves. Some way of saying *I am here. I am here. I am.* One stone for each of the heart's old brags. But it looks like some of the stones have other, deeper meanings. One toppled cairn is strewn with white flowers, the petals old and fragile. There's an empty bottle of perfume too. Perhaps this place was special to someone they loved. They wanted to think of them in a place with big views, where they would always see them. I don't know. Perhaps it was not the view but the fog that made them place stone on stone. I think in the closed-in world of fog a cairn makes sense; it is smaller and more personal. There is a greater sense of ownership in that little circle of visibility. I'm not sure that holds when light floods back in, laying bare this private corner to the rest of the world once more.

Over Hope Valley, the sun is breaking through fog that has become, for the most part, low cloud. The sun's rays are clearly visible in this watery light. They are crepuscular, angled into water droplets and highlighting three trees that stand in an otherwise unremarkable patch of field. They are gilded now. Glowing. I wonder what it would be like to stand there. Would you notice? Would you just think the chill of the fog had lifted? That the sun had finally come out? Would you realise that the sun was shining only on you? I look east again, past Back Tor to the hump of Losehill, the last peak of the Great Ridge. The fog is still blowing that way, collecting in drifts behind it. I start to shuffle down the tor, heading towards it.

As I'm nearing Castleton, my phone pings with a weather warning. The app I open says there will be more fog tonight. The report talks of it disappearing but quickly reforming – more battleground semantics. There seems to be a rhythm to the fog here, coming and going as if the land is breathing. In fact, if there is a lesson that fog has taught me, it is one about constantly shifting rhythms. How there is a miracle at play in the factors that make it. A miracle in experiencing it arrive and depart.

It's hard not to fall into a trap with fog, to describe it in terms that are laden with baggage. To ghost it up. To talk about how it is wraith-like and create a landscape of Dickens or Stevenson. But it is definitely different from other experiences. With the rain, whether it was the towering size of the clouds, the movement of them towards me, or the feel of drops hitting bare skin, there was a hint of the sublime. But standing in the fog I didn't think like that once. There is a cosiness to it that persists despite the chill it can put in your bones. But watching its retreat, the transition from smoke to burning brightness, really has the power to enthral. Suddenly the world is solid again, familiar, no trace of the eeriness that touched every aspect of the landscape just moments ago. It's as if that ethereal world never existed.

ICE AND SNOW

Winter is on its way. The mellow softness of autumn is to give way to hard angles. Sharp crystals and even sharper frosts.

Snow is transformative; it has the power to make even the most humdrum landscapes and objects into something of rare beauty. It changes sound, creates light, insists that we react, touch and feel. Deep snow, the snow of play and perfect Christmases, is – and has been for some time – a weather of rarity in the UK. When it does arrive, we need no encouragement to rush outside and embrace it.

Without it, wintry weather holds less appeal: the deep freezes with skies that pale into nothingness; the days when the sun is muffled by a fog that turns roads and paths into death traps; those times when the cold wriggles its way into our bones like worms into wood. I know that I have often looked out of the window and decided to stay in. The ice and freeze have been problems to be navigated and over-come rather than to be encountered in any meaningful way. But if fog has taught me anything, it is that even when our world shrinks to almost nothing, a quiet magic envelops us, if we only stop to notice it. Ice, I'm sure, will hold its own enchantments as it claims the land, water and sky.

HALOS. HOAR FROST. ICE MAPS.
December, Bury St Edmunds

When the fog disappears, it is like a retreating tide, leaving a sky that is washed out and pale. The day feels glassy and exposed. As if the sea had rolled back too far. Had shown too much. The temperature drops and when I get up for work, the windscreen is feathered in ice. I put the wipers on and watch the patterns change, see the ice turn somersaults and disappear.

The weather grows colder still throughout the day, the sky blue and brittle with it. The evening brings the cold moon of December that shines through high cirrus clouds that are soft with snow but also steely with ice. The moonlight bounces off the hexagonal ice in the atmosphere to create a halo, faintly coloured. The bright, scratchy light, like lines etched in glass, takes on a petrol tint.

Halos were once used as a weather tell. A way to forecast before the development of modern meteorology. And it is true: the icy cirrus clouds that commonly form halos do often signify that a frontal system is approaching. But that is all. Fronts can be inactive or change direction without producing a drop of precipitation. Later that night I check the TV forecast: the movement of lines, cold triangles and the white starred symbols for snow. The presenter smiles and says the mild air has gone, replaced by air from a cold northerly flow. He waves a hand over the thin neck of Scotland, his fingers tracing a path down the spine of the Pennines. There's a greater risk of wintry showers in places in northern England, especially over high ground. Minimum temperatures over the next few days are expected to drop below freezing, heightening the risk of some ice formation. Better wrap up warm, he says.

The forecast is right. The cold hardens. Grows its scales over the car windscreen. After the strange warmth of autumn, the change is almost startling. Our house grows cold quickly. There are multiple ways in for draughts and chills: through the back door where the dog, in her maddening teen years, scratched a hole that we swear we'll fix every winter; through the single panes of the sash windows that knock with the wind and bleed coldness through the glass; through the floorboards that are suspended a foot above cold, compacted earth. In our house, a lit candle doesn't know which way to dance. We wrap ourselves in jumpers and blankets, rummage in the shed for offcuts of wood to burn. Then, teeth gritted with the thought of the bill, we turn the heating up by an extra click.

It's Sunday morning and the sun is up and muffled. It is a pure white, cold circle, like a Communion host ready to be placed on a tongue. The light is silvery, like moonlight. It falls hard on the grass, turns all that was once green to glinting cold metal. We are walking along a narrow strip that forms a public footpath near Felsham. To the left are the ash and hazel coppices of Bradfield Woods. To the right is farmland marked out by thick shaggy-backed hedges. The field is dotted with a few veteran trees that once would have been in the middle of the wood – the survivors of grubbing and burning that took place in the 1960s when the government decided fields held more value than ancient wood. This field has just been emptied, perhaps in a rush to beat the weather. The soil is tamped down tight and herringboned with the wide print of tractor tyres. By the entrance sugar beet has been piled into 2-metre mounds the shape of long barrows.

The air is perfectly still and our breath forms clouds around our faces. The moisture beads on our scarves and snoods, turning from hot to cold against our lips. Our own little dew points. Jen holds up her phone, wiggles it at me, says that it is showing as −2°C, but it feels colder on bare skin. The cold got into my hands when I took my gloves off to take photos. It slipped into the ink of the tattoos on my fingers. Redrew them again and again until the patterns burned and throbbed like picked scabs.

The message that Seth's football match had been

cancelled arrived early this morning. Sorry, everyone; the pitch is frozen. No game today. Have a lovely weekend. We read it while we were still in bed with the dog, the dry heat of her pads resting on my thigh. The first cup of tea, still hot enough to scald. It had been tempting to stay there and hunker down but there was something about the light coming through the window. If nothing else, we said, the house will feel a bit warmer when we return.

Lyra was unsure about the walk at first. Grumpy in her coat, she had pulled on her lead to go back to the car. But now she is off and running, doing a mad ears-back skittery dash across the field, before looping back and going again. We follow her, wondering if she's excited to be out or just moving fast to reduce the time her paws are in contact with the frozen ground. The land around here is always wet: Bradfield Woods is itself a wet woodland, and the River Lark, a winterbourne chalk stream, rises nearby.

Now the puddles have been turned to a slightly fogged glass, patterned with pearl-white whorls that remind me of feathered icing. When I step off the path, I find the panes are thick and strong. The smallest puddles take my weight completely, with only the widest singing and cracking under the heels of my boots. But the soil itself is not frosted; like sand it radiates heat quickly but also gains heat quickly from deeper underground, meaning it is not cold enough for dew and frost. The only sign of frost today is on fallen, blown leaves from the wood and on the few forgotten sugar beets that have been frozen into the mud, their hard sides marked and scooped by deer teeth.

Frost forms the same way as dew, but when the air is cold enough, the water vapour freezes to ice crystals and forms hoar frost. Once you get your eye in, hoar frost is a map. A chart of temperature and light. There are clear contours of coldness, both on the ground and in the air. A hand close to the soil is colder than one above our head. The haws on the outer edge of the treeline are sugared; the ones higher up are not. For dew and then frost to form, heat needs to be able to radiate all the way into a clear sky. Across the medieval ditches that form the boundaries of the woodland, the frost thins and disappears. The heat must have been trapped under the wood's mantling branches.[*]

The more we look, the more we see; the more we riddle out the movements of air. Frost here, but not under there. We can see it gripping this plant, but not that one. Eighteenth-century naturalist Gilbert White, a man of the weather, wrote in *The Natural History of Selborne* how fossilised wood was found in bogs by following the maps of hoar frost, 'which lay longer over the space where they were concealed, than on the surrounding morass'. He noticed too that snow 'continued to lie' where there were drains as it

---

[*] T. Gooley, *The Secret World of Weather* (Sceptre, 2021) contains some excellent ways to read weather.

'intercepted the warmth of the earth from ascending from greater depths below them'.

We are walking slowly now, bending to inspect grass that has almost been thorned by ice, dewdrop upon frozen dew-drop. Nearby is a plant that has been rendered unidentifiable by pine needles of ice, the crystals bristling like guard-hairs. Guard hoars: the word is derived from the Middle English *hor*, meaning grey or white-haired. Jen stops by a patch of long grass, with its blades locked into a droop by ice that appears to have built outwards like coral polyps. The dog is frustrated at our pace. She loops around us in consterna-tion, paws clicking over ice puddles, crunching over grass, her prints leaving darker patches in the map of ice. Her circles get tighter and tighter the slower we go, as if she is trying to lasso us with movement, to round us up and drag us along with her.

I had taken my gloves off again to touch the hoars and discovered that the cold has teeth. Even now, with the gloves back on, I can feel it biting into bone; the veins closing up, the blood thick and sluggish. I rub them together. Flap them about. Jen says her feet are cold too – she can no longer feel the bend of her toes. Someone we know trekked across the Antarctic. He told us how he hadn't noticed the skin on three of his toes had gone paler, and had been relieved when they'd stopped burning. He snapped them off when they went black and keeps at least one of them inside a glass paperweight.

We stop at the corner, where the length of the field ends in rough bird cover that runs all the way to the tree line. The sun, straight in front of us, is partly strained through tree branches, but the light glares hard off the frost. The matt silver of moonlight has been replaced with a smashed-mirror spark and glint. Frost and brightness seem to go together, its angular crystals holding the light across all their faces.

Jen is looking in a different direction. She pulls my hand and points. *Look. Look.* A hare is streaking across the field, running hard. I think we are too far away to have spooked it into such a sprint but it is really shifting. We watch it eat up the frozen ground, its hind legs almost striking its glued-back ears, until it goes through a knot of rooks that rises in confusion and we lose track of it. I'd like to keep going, to try to find the hare's tracks in the frost. To sense a trace of her in those darkened footsteps. But the dog has had enough. We turn back, heading for home and an ash fire, the dog pausing with a raised paw every time ice drops from a branch.

FEN SKATERS. BLACK ICE. ELATION.
Welney and Sutton, December

I see the skater on Welney Wash as soon as I cross the New Bedford river. A dark figure against ice that looks like an extension of the sky. All greys and powdery blues, the odd dark patch of ice where undergrowth from the meadow presses closer to the surface or where yesterday's snow has been blown away. I pull in the car and watch. The man – I can see now it is a man – moves his whole body as he drives towards me, his knees following the swing of his arms. I can hear the grind of his blades as he gathers speed – a bit like a carving knife drawn against a steel. He lowers his hockey stick, flicks a puck with one side, then the other. The touches, although delicate – light, like fingers dancing over a just-come-out-of-the-oven heat – ring with a hollow, wood-on-wood clack that slides out over the fen. The skater corners, swerves around grass that still peeks through the freeze. The blades of his skates rasp up a horseshoe of white powder. Then there is the grind again as the blades bite and he pushes off, back out to where the ice stretches to the ice-rimed scrub and low trees whose branches are bright white against a white sky. I wonder how far the freeze stretches from there. One mile? Two? Three? A thick glaze that reaches all the way to the Wash? The thought of it is oddly thrilling, as if suddenly a whole new world has been formed: a flat Narnia on East Anglia's rump.

There has been ice skating in the Fens for centuries. The conditions that made it possible are a side effect of the drainage that was designed to tame this place, to bend wild marshland into productive farmland: to straighten it out; to beat it flat and peaty black. When the Bedford, which partly channelled the great outflows of the Ouse, was deemed insufficient in the seventeenth century, another 'river', the New

Bedford, was cut a short distance away. Two lead-coloured parallel lines that carried the water to the Wash. But the land between the rivers, a parcel around a kilometre wide and 24 kilometres in length, was low and prone to flooding. And if the water was at the right depth and if the cold set in hard enough, if it lingered long enough, the washes and meadows froze.

With the agricultural work that dominated the region impossible in the frozen conditions, the fenlanders emptied out onto the ice. Long blades, known as fen runners, were attached to working boots and men, women and children flocked to the ice. It was a skating of leisure, of freedom, a chance to reclaim the landscape they once moved so freely over, but it was also taken seriously. They raced around fenland courses marked with barrels and posts in championships, for village pride, for money or for sides of meat that were hung outside pubs; it's there the long-gone winners live on today, in beery breath and black-and-white photographs, the old-fashioned flash leaving the men's irises over-exposed and glowing pale like ice.

In the Fens, the champion skaters of the nineteenth century are still folk heroes. There is William Smart, from Welney, known as 'Turkey' Smart for pioneering the arms-behind-back, chest-out-like-a-farmyard-bird pose now adopted by so many skaters. Then there are his sons, George 'Flying Fish' and James; his brother-in-law Gutta Percha and his son young Gutty. Larman Register, the 'big

Littleport man' of the 1850s, who, so the story goes, once raced a train between Littleport and Ely for a bet. Despite his competitors' attempts to melt the ice by throwing cinders from a bridge, Register still made it home 30 seconds in front.

Engravings created in the 1820s show huge crowds gathered on the ice, similar to the frost fairs of the Thames. Londoners came to watch the fenlanders skate, with as many as 4,000 people going through the turnstiles at Littleport station. In 1879 The National Skating Association was formed in Cambridge and took the top few fen skaters to the Netherlands, where in 1895 James Smart became Britain's only ever world champion speed skater. Ice is a part of this place; it has crept under the skin of its people.

I walk to the edge where rough grass slowly becomes smooth ice, the creeping flood waters frozen just a few feet from the road. Standing next to the ice, the temperature seems lower. It is a cold of sharp edges. The kind that burns your nostrils and makes your eyes water. Yesterday was the coldest day of the year. The coldest in the UK since December 2010. In Braemar, Aberdeenshire, the daytime temperature didn't rise above −9.3°C. Last night it was −17.3°C. In England the temperature was higher, but still a record low for 2022 with the coldest measurement being −11.8°C at Redesdale in Northamptonshire. The media has been talking of Arctic blasts. The articles I have read explained how northerly winds have been forced south between high- and low-pressure systems. The highs have been reinforced. They have formed a 'blocking pattern'.

I'm not sure I grasp the science, but I understand the cold. I have felt how it has mantled the house, how it has blown up through the gaps in the floorboards, under the front door, through the cat flap and scratched its way through the thin glass of our windows. Technically it is heat that exits rather than cold that gets in, but this cold feels active. Something that clicks its claws on the floor and tiles. We've been forced into wearing multiple layers and squabbling over who gets to cuddle the dog as the boiler whoomphs and wheezes with effort. We go to bed early to read under thick duvets. The character in the book I'm reading goes to sleep listening to the sound of a frozen river, the bangs and cracks of it echoing around her room. I have the central heating instead, clicking and purring, whining like too much blood in the ears. The radiators coughing bubbles.

To be honest, the thought of going outside was not all that appealing. But I've always wanted to see the fen skaters, and with the promise of a perfect icy landscape to explore, all week I have been tracking the skaters on social media. As soon as the cold hardened, there were whispers about conditions having potential. Two or three more days of cold and the ice could be thick enough. There is consensus that this year it could happen. Details are exchanged about pubs with rooms, about railways and their distances from favourite haunts – the Welney Wash, Sutton. Then, last night, there were photos and videos. Four men, locked into a starting position, on ice that looks like black marble, its surface scarred with the white traces of speed skates. Their faces are images of pure joy. A racer leaning into a corner as he races around a telegraph pole that leans back in the opposite direction, anchored in the ice. A girl, leaning forward, one leg raised parallel with her body, as if she is dancing the geometry of the Fens, expressing the right angles of road, dyke and ditch while gliding on a few millimetres of steel. The next morning I aimed the car towards that strip of land between man-made rivers to watch those who have truly embraced the ice.

As the Welney skater brakes and sprays more powdered ice into the air, I ask if he minds me taking pictures. 'Go for it,' he says. A photographer, down on one knee by the side of the ice, is already clicking away. His name is Martin and when he looks up we realise we know each other, have worked together on a photoshoot about canoeing and rivers. We had both come here on the off chance of seeing skaters take to the ice. At the edge, where the ice-blasted grass and thistle give way to the thick glaze of the frozen washes, the ice is still relatively thin. It cracks like burnt sugar under a spoon. The skater, whose name is Sammy, is wearing dark-blue jeans, a navy top and thick orange gloves. His eyes are hidden behind dark glasses. When I look at him all I see is a reflection of the ice staring back. His voice is soft, deep and gently North American. The thickness of the ice, he says, is on the 'absolute limit' for skating.

'My skates have gone in a few times, at the edge it is under an inch, but up here . . .' he skates away, scratch, scratch, slide, spray; uses his hockey stick to hammer at the ice and extract a wedge. He slides it towards me, the shard tinkling like a wind chime. It's about three inches, he says. Four inches is better. But it's easier to skate than walk on it. Better grip for one – the skate is like a knife, its teeth grabbing hold of the ice. Also with skates your lead foot is always dragging you forward; your body travels faster than the ice breaks.

The snow has changed the feel of the ice, turning the black, smooth freeze milky. When I've swum in deep lakes and lochs you can feel the texture of the water changing, its willingness to hold you up disappear with the bite of cold that shivers over those deepest, darkest points. It feels almost like the opposite of an air thermal. To ride it would mean a spiral into the depths. I like the idea that the ice, too, holds a record of the changing weather – freeze and fall – in its texture: days, hours and minutes locked in cold crystal. I also like the irony that the cold now holds up instead of dragging down. I venture a bit further out, baby steps. Trying to resist the urge to tiptoe, which would put more pressure on a single point of the ice. The surface crunches, cracks, sings, but holds.

I ask Sammy how the ice of the Fens got in his veins.

He smiles, turns back to me. 'I met these guys, who are like the evangelists of ice-skating, when I was roller-skating on the Guided Busway near St Ives and they were on these speed skates. We were going in opposite directions and they told me what happened in the Fens.

'A lot of people pray for warmth, but for me, when it's like this, I want it to go the other way. I understand those people – my wife is at home with a blanket and a hot-water bottle – but this is where I've got to be.'

I leave him to practise, but instead of heading back to the car, I walk between the cracking tideline of the ice and the field's boundaries. I took my gloves off to take pictures and my fingers now feel swollen and painful, as if something has been inserted into the joints, pushing apart the bone. But being cold outside is different from being cold inside. Perhaps part of it is our expectation. Humans adapt their environments to their needs, to their demand for comfort; when the cold invades our shelters it is unsettling, unwelcome. But outside, when we're trussed up and ready for it, there is something invigorating about the frigid temperature.

I stop at a frozen drainage ditch the colour of lead and turn back to get a view of the wash. Behind me, the sun is as high as it will get and the whole landscape winks with light. Sparks with cold. Ice-covered poplars stand tall like teeth on a comb. Above the dyke I can see the roof of a house, the windows of its upper storey peeking over. And out on the ice Sammy is still there, dribbling his puck, moving over the surface with a smoothness that is not of the land.

It is two hours later and I have driven thirty minutes to Sutton Gault, where Sammy said he was meeting other skaters. He insists they have a feeling for the ice. A tingling. They can scent it in the air. But they also have a WhatsApp group that grows active when the water grows sludgy with cold. There is no one here yet.

The road was marshalled with gates that close when there is high water. There are floodline numbers. The gault is low-lying land. Even the name is wet. Gault. Gulp. It means something like 'thick, heavy clay'. I stand on a raised metal walkway that runs parallel to a road I later find out is called the causeway. From here I can see a fair distance over the flooded and frozen fen. The ditch that separates the road from fen ditch is fringed with reeds that have snapped under the weight of ice. Beyond that are fence posts, and a wallpaper-paste grey stretch of ice that is patterned with thin crusts of snow. Where the snow has been moved by the wind the ice looks darker. Deeper.

The freezing fog that has hovered over the Fens for most of the day hasn't lifted and, if anything, is thickening as it's stirred by the lightest and coldest of breezes. I can't work out how far the ice stretches. To the trees that I can just

make out? Further? I keep walking along the causeway. Up
and down. It's too cold to stay still. Plus, after feeling so
enchanted with the idea of a landscape of ice this morning,
I'm now feeling strangely unnerved by it. I think it is the
noiselessness of it. Here, on my own, the silence has a heaviness to it that makes me want to shake my head to dislodge
it, like water after the swimming pool. I want to chase it
away by clanging my feet on the walkway.

Martin pulls up in his car and lowers a window. He says
he's driven up and down and hasn't seen anyone either. He
keeps the engine running while I try to get closer to the ice,
following heron prints in frozen snow up a flooded trackway where the ice has been smashed into inch-thick panes.
Walking on the ice is different from looking at it. Each footstep crunches with the music of breaking glass and I get
sucked into the sound of it, forcing my toes and then heels
down harder and harder to change the tone. My feet are
aching with the cold. I climb through a gap in a fence where
brambles have grown long, white, rimed needles and stand
on the thin edge of fen ice that creaks and cracks but does
not give. The sun is still up behind the mist but it is just a
white orb in the sky, surrounded by the slight glimmer of
a corona. I listen to the ice, the gentle song of it, and watch
my breath rising away from me.

I retrace my steps back to Martin as another car arrives.
This time it's Sammy, waving enthusiastically. The back of
his car is a jumble of ice-hockey goals and sticks. It is the

first time he has been here too. We walk back along the road and stand at a fence staring at a landscape that is impossibly thick with cold. The Fens are always wide open. It is a place of horizons. Of flatness running towards the sky. But it feels as though the weather has exaggerated things further, as if the ice has grown in the thin crack between land and air. Lifting the sky higher, like frozen milk forced from a glass bottle.

Martin wonders if the dark patterns that zigzag across the landscape are patches where the ice has melted. But Sammy isn't so sure. Possibly wind patterns caused by blown snow, or maybe even just the blackness of ice, where the snow didn't freeze onto the surface.

A dark shape catches my eye. Some way off. Almost like a fisherman's fly being played out over the surface of still water. I point at a spot to the right of a telegraph pole and we look again. There is the lean. The hands behind the back. The turkey chest pointing towards the frosted trees. A skater.

We walk back along the causeway and turn right by the Anchor, a pub where only the top windows of its long, cream building peak above the embankment of the New Bedford. The Hundred Foot Drain. The river, despite its straightness, its apparent lack of flow, is free of ice and stretches with the fields as far as the eye can see. It is a technical drawing of a landscape. All angles and rulers. Calculations that have been made strange by nature. The ground is like iron on the embankment between field and water. A line of old snow, caught in the dip between path and embankment, follows the water west: two lines that never meet, fusing on the horizon. On the other side of the path the ice stretches out far into the distance. Now we are closer, we can see that although the wind has whipped some of the snow from the surface, there are also more standardised patterns. It marks the edges of drains and fields, places where the vegetation has slowed the already minimal heat rising up from the ground.

We can see the skater more clearly now. We can get a sense of the speed he's going, hear the crinkling of the blades, the emery-board rasp of every corner taken at speed as a hand flicks out from behind his back, perhaps to give balance, perhaps to give extra propulsion.

There is a gap at the first tree line and another in the reeds that leads down to the ice. By the time we reach him, the skater has stopped and is sitting on a small plastic stool that is set about four or five feet out on the ice. His bag is next to him along with a pair of sheepskin-lined boots. I ask if it's OK to walk out to him without skates on. He raises a hand in greeting and then points at where to avoid – tufts of grass that form neat lines across the ice mark the edge of the deep drainage ditch.

'Avoid the snow. You never really know what it covers,' he says in a warm voice, the words burred and horned like ice.

The skater's name is Richard. He's wearing a black woollen hat kept in place with a chin strap. His eyes are dark, almond-shaped, and twinkling behind a pair of black-framed goggles. The snow around him is covered in bird tracks. One large, scuffing its feet, so the steps are joined with dark lines; next to them a smaller, thinner trail of prints that look like crosses or the silhouettes of jet fighters flying in single file.

I tell him how graceful he looked from the path, how easy and fluid his movements were. I realise that I'm dancing around the fact that I am surprised that he is not a young man. He smiles as he looks up from retying his skates, the lines around his eyes and mouth deepening.

When pressed, he says that he once raced in the World Masters Championship and came second in a Fen Championship, but is modest to the point of shyness. 'It was way back, probably a fluke. In terms of good skaters, I'm rubbish, but in terms of fen skaters, I'm OK.' Richard moves differently off the ice. Carefully, deliberately. The kind of movement that comes with age. I ask if it feels like freedom being on the ice.

'Oh, yes. It's strange. I'm seventy-eight, but as I get closer to the ice I find my foot on the accelerator goes a bit . . . harder. I move easier too. It's a fluid movement. It's habit. I probably won't get up the stairs to bed tonight.' Richard says his wife stays at home now, but she skates well too. Some of their first dates were out on the ice. It is hard to think of anything more romantic. The smoothness of movement, the cold outside and the warmth generated from skating. The magic of spontaneity, the freezing of time.

Another one of the old guard has arrived. Dave is bigger-framed and younger than Richard. He drops his bag down and gets out skates that have a thin gold blade, a world away from the agricultural fen runners. He says he has come straight from work. He called in some of the ice holidays that he saves up every year. The excitement these men clearly feel as the cold days creep in feels akin to how I waited, as a child, for the first snow to fall.

Richard turns, walking stiffly through a gap in the snow, keeping the exposed, rimed undergrowth that marks the twin lines of the ditch to his right – places where the water, should the ice break, is deep enough to submerge you. As he reaches the corner of the skating ice his footsteps become wider, until he is push-gliding away, a hand coming up behind his back. Dave follows him, testing the blades or testing the ice, or both, and then he too is off. Pushing hard with his legs, barrel chest forward, his arms swinging him forwards faster and faster before they are both tucked in by the time he reaches the first corner. Sammy breaks away from his circles and tight turns that send up little smoke signals of ice and races to catch up, until he falls into formation. I can hear Martin's camera clicking off shots.

I wish I had skates, that I could feel the ice like them. Because I have no doubt that they are feeling it, their movements guided by instinct rather than land-locked logic. But it was also magical to see them skate. To see them transformed by the ice, their elation unmistakable. They were moving differently, full of a grace that is not associated with late middle age; with frozen joints, with aches and pain and the threats of crumbling bones. As they corner, their rhythms come together so it looks as if they are dancing. It is bewitching, a kind of studied thoughtlessness.

As they come towards us the sound increases: a grinding, gritty, creaky crackling that doesn't match the smoothness of their movements. Something solid meets something hollow. Dave is in front now. Stooped forward in the Turkey Smart pose, arms behind back. His legs too have a poultry quality, a scratching kick that propels him at speed. Richard comes alongside him. The same posture. It gives them a look of intense seriousness. As if they are lawyers in a courtroom conflab.

As the skaters keep going, lap after lap, swaying and leaning into corners, a skein of geese, greylag I think from the sound of them, flies over like an arrow pointing north. I walk a bit on the ice. To feel a part of it. The ice sings underneath me. Richard had already told me to keep shifting. Don't leave your weight for too long in one place. As at Welney, the ice is still thin, they say. Two inches. But it will do. I shift my weight again and the ice grumbles. Richard said the Fens were really a glorified puddle. That as long as you don't wander onto a dyke you'll get nothing worse than a wet foot. It is strange being suspended by frozen water, but there is no transformation for my body – it remains upright, my limbs don't fold into a lean perfected over a lifetime of winters.

I stay and talk as they continue their laps, my questions asked and answered in rotations. The words chipped off like ice and thrown back to me. I've heard that the way fenlanders speak is also born of weather: their words forced through teeth clenched against easterlies that have blown in from the frigid Russian steppes. When the guys do stop, I ask them about the first time they skated. All of them remember it clearly and it's hard not to share their joy. It is a memory that has been recalled again and again, smoothed and polished by attention. It was in the evening, after their dads returned from work with borrowed skates. They were carried or given piggybacks to the ice, told to watch and learn before taking their first strides, their first push, push glides on moonlit ice.

As they talk, it's hard not to think of time. For both of the older skaters, the memory of those first skates is hoary with age but still as clear as ice. I wonder if it's as easy to recall when the weather is not like this. Does the light aid the memory? The cold fire up the synapses? Does the body say, I remember, I remember? Does the brain recall the details in the same way as the foot that instinctively pushes, the back that leans? Perhaps the gap between their first and last skate is not a matter of decades but a few details: a goose call, the sound of a blade on snow ice, the cold that creeps out of the bones. Dave catches me staring out at the ice and smiles broadly.

'It's beautiful, isn't it?'

I smile back. It really is.

An hour passes. Then another. I don't want to leave. But I've got the school run to do. I think about the logistics of getting the kids and then driving back here. As I'm leaving, there are others arriving. A woman called Verity sits down on the ice to do her boots up. She is flushed from the cold, or maybe from running while carrying her daughter – a girl of about two who is crying loudly and wearing so many clothes her arms stick out at right angles. Verity talks over her, explaining how she is here because she knows Sammy, that today will be only her second time on fen ice. Her very first was last night, when she skated under the Cold Moon. Her face changes as she tells me how beautiful the light was, the frost and the ice a pure, glittering white.

As I walk to the car I think back on Richard's words about the excitement of ice. How even in his late seventies he finds his foot pushing the accelerator that little bit harder as he gets closer to the frozen washes. Still chasing the ice and understanding more than ever how these moments need to be seized and savoured.

WHITE CHRISTMAS. FIRST SNOW.
Isle of Skye, December

We are spending Christmas in a cottage on the north-west coast of Skye. A cabin down the end of a track that was more hole than road and clonked the underbelly of our Mini. It is wood-clad and warm, with a clear view of the sea from the window. On the first morning I wake early to the dark that presses up against the windows. The wind is whistling, causing something to flap. The train of air sounds eerily like the thrum of the A14 that you can hear from most points of Bury St Edmunds. I light a fire that is sucked hot up the chimney and wait for light to give me purchase on the day.

From the front of the cottage, you face east towards Varkasaig beach – a sharp horn of black sand sitting in a bay that from the air looks like the silhouette of a sheep's head – and the tidal waters of Loch Barcasaid. There is a system of dry-stone walls, frosted with white lichen and tussocks of grass, the quills of sedge. To the right, crossing the burn that feeds rain and meltwater into the sea loch, is a thick sweep of pines that closes over a path tracking around the bay's southern edge. Straight out, at the neck of the bay, the waves run in fast from the open water, throwing themselves into the low-lying heaps of kelp-covered rocks, exploding spume with the sound of a handclap in an empty room.

It was the wind that pulled me here, that justified the

twelve-hour drive with four of us and a dog, our friends James and Anna in another car, but there is other weather incoming. Two nights ago, we had broken our journey in Carlisle. We had drunk beers and Cokes out of bottles and looked up at TV screens that showed a yellow splodge spreading over the Highlands and the Islands. The subtitles had stuttered. Struggled to keep up. There was a yellow warning for ice and snow being pushed into the north by a south-westerly, and rain with gales in the south. After the hard edges of ice, I am ready for the softness of snow.

Snow often follows a cold snap. The clouds of a front mean higher temperatures rather than clear skies; they also mean precipitation. When the icy wind warms, expect snowstorms. Jen loves saying it's too cold for snow. The subtitles posed the question of a white Christmas. The presenter continues to talk, but the same question stays on the screen even after the camera cuts away from the presenter. The answer never appears.

As we drove north the next day we could see that the thaw from the past two weeks of freezing temperatures has taken longer up here. I guess the wind had further to go, its mildness dulled by the time it had swept over so much cold ground. In the Highlands the old snow was still heaped at the roadside. Rotten-looking, frozen and stained, but there all right. On the peaks at Glencoe and on the Cuillins the snow lay in bones, packed into the pits and grooves of the rockface like white greasepaint in open pores.

It is evening and Christmas Day has burned bright and short. The darkness fell away at nine and rose again just after two. In the morning we had run down to the sea and swum in water so cold it had made breathing hard. As if the air was a hard pill we couldn't quite swallow. Afterwards we had wrapped ourselves in towels and drunk Buck's Fizz out of wine glasses that were rimmed with black sand. We danced to keep warm, slapping our arms and legs until it formed an accidental rhythm we all joined. The wind pulled at our hair and whipped away our laughter. For the rest of the day we glowed. We sat around a table lit by candles and played games and opened presents. We ate and drank, and when in the late afternoon the light went out with the tide, James and I went outside with the children and piled split pine logs into the fire pit.

Seth and Eliza tell jokes and roast marshmallows while James and I stretch our hands out towards the flames. We have been watching the skies for the frost of stars but there is a growing haze now. A cloud cover that is the same colour as the smoke that drifts towards the beach. Our breath is smoking too. All day we had been talking about the possibility of snow, sneaking glimpses at weather apps, peering at the sky. Jen had reminded me about an old friend in Brighton who would, without fail, get an upset stomach if it was going to snow. He called it his snow feeling. We would text his wife as soon as the weather turned cold. Waiting with bated breath for the response. But still, when the snow starts it's a surprise.

At first it comes widely spaced and then falling with a gathering speed. The children raise their faces from the fire, up to a dark that is flecked with white, watching thick snow-flakes fall down. They have the consistency of cake crumbs. Eliza stands head back, tongue out. Joyous. Managing to laugh at the same time. We laugh too. The simple joy of snow and of all that it signifies. Play. Purity. Simplicity. The peace of Christmas, the swaddling cold of it.

Snow has something nostalgic to it. It generates flashes of memories. A red plastic sled. A woodland somewhere in Essex where the branches formed snowy archways across the rides, the sound of wheels turning endlessly on the hill where we once lived. But I don't think I can remember a single white Christmas.

The phrase 'white Christmas' has become almost a bless-ing, an integral part of a Christmas experience in popular imagination. When I was young, I remember watching a TV programme where people with relatives in Australia would talk to each other via satellite link. My mum would say she wouldn't want to have a hot Christmas; it wouldn't feel right. But the greyness of most of my Christmas skies didn't feel right either. It seemed as though the world should transform for Christmas. It should sparkle.

The chances of having snow at Christmas are, just like

all weather, dependent on where you live. The definition of a white Christmas is geographically specific too. In the USA, there has to be at least 2.5 centimetres of snow on the ground in states that share a common border, while in the Great White North of Canada, a white Christmas is one where there is more than 2 centimetres on the ground on 25 December. In the UK, the definition provided by the Met Office (and used by the bookmakers) is for snow to be observed falling – regardless of how much, or even any, is on the ground. There might be drifts of snow on the ground, but unless a single flake is seen to fall, it does not constitute a white Christmas.

Scotland, particularly the north-east, is the most likely to see a white Christmas in the UK. Here it has happened in thirty-seven years since 1960, compared with sixteen in Northern Ireland and sixteen in Wales. The north of England has had twenty-six during that same period, while the warmer south has seen just ten. While having a white Christmas doesn't necessarily mean you'd have enough to form a snowball, let alone a blanket, that doesn't mean the UK has never seen deep snow. In 1981, the deepest lying snow recorded was measured at 47 centimetres in Kindrogan, Perthshire. The Welsh record, made in 2010, is 45 centimetres at Cae Poeth, Gwynedd. In England 43 centimetres was recorded at Buxton, Derbyshire and Malham Tarn, in North Yorkshire, in the frigid winters of 1981 and 2009.

But why is the association between snow and Christmas so strong? In all likelihood, this nostalgia for something we have never really experienced is rooted in the traditional artwork, literature and music that were formed during what has become known as the Little Ice Age. Spanning a period from the early fourteenth century through to the mid-nineteenth, the Little Ice Age was a time of unusually cold weather in the Northern Hemisphere that saw temperatures drop by around 0.6°C relative to the mean between 1000 and 2000 CE. Over this time, pack ice in the northern Atlantic grew, as did glaciers, while rivers, including the Thames, froze. Woollen underpants were developed. Chimneys were built. Hypothermia, famine and poverty increased – in fact the rise of witch-hunting episodes in Europe has been linked to the agricultural failures and desperation of the Little Ice Age. The climatologist Henry Lamb suggests that in many years, 'snowfall was much heavier than recorded before or since, and the snow lay on the ground for many months longer than it does today'. It was during this time that Charles Dickens, born at the frosty tail end of the Little Ice Age, wrote *A Christmas Carol*. The novella – which shaped so much about how we see Christmas, from its listing of foods to its descriptions of celebrations and goodwill – is also notable for its weather: the figurative and literal scorching cold. Dickens' biographer Peter Ackroyd would later suggest that our imagery of a snowy Christmas could be considered to be 'a mere accident of history' – a result of the fact that

Dickens would have experienced a white Christmas for the first eight years of his life.

We call for Jen and Anna who are curled up on sofas in the house as the snow grows in strength but still doesn't settle on the wet stone around the cottage, on the salt-sprayed black of the beach. Stronger, until the snow is not a white streak past the light, but so thick you can no longer look up without getting snow in your eyes, meshing and melting in eyelashes, each unique crystal bleeding out. And then it stops.

SNOW SWIM. LETHARGY.
Isle of Skye, December

There is snow on the wind's breath as we start down the trail towards the river. The path is a dark wiggling line across the copper wash of the moorland that connects with the other thicker dark line of the River Brittle. Above it, the Cuillins rise gigantic and toothy and elephant-skinned, the cracks and folds of its black gabbro rocks packed with snow. It makes me think of barnacle crusts, or old whales that have been scarred white by deep-sea battles with squid or slashed by ship propellers. There is something of the heaved-from-the-sea about this part of Skye. As if it is only a temporary breaching and that one day it will wake and shake and sink again.

It is Boxing Day and James, Anna and I have driven across the island to swim at the fairy pools near Glenbrittle: a system of glacier-carved waterfalls where the pools are deep, clear and cold. Although it is only about 40 kilometres from the cottage – when the clouds rise we can see the Cuillins in the distance, bared like knuckles – the drive had taken over an hour as the roads narrowed and became slick with ice and snow. It is still early afternoon but as we head down the trail with our towels under our arms, most of the walkers appear to be heading in the opposite direction. James points at the clouds that seem to be lowering overhead. The sky has turned the colour of old ash.

The snow begins to fall as James and I are looking for ways down into one of the pools. Thick, fluffy, downy flakes. A feathery snow that furs our clothes and hangs on the black sides of the rock before disappearing, as if it is somehow worming its way inside. The pool is probably deep enough to plunge into, but I don't want to risk it. The idea of submerging so quickly is not appealing. The water is calling, though. I don't think I've ever seen natural water so strangely, ethereally blue. I know it is caused by reflections and light bouncing from mineral-rich rock, but still it holds a magic that fits with the snow. We find a narrow route down through rocks that are so cold they feel as if they will stick to the skin, and stand on a narrow ledge about a foot above the water. The river flows along a narrow corridor of rock before turning sharply into a deep pool that undercuts a cliff-like boulder. The water drops smoothly down to the pool below, creating a perfectly still infinity pool whose surface is dimpled only by the falling snow.

We undress quietly and quickly, shooting quick grins up at Anna standing above us. The mountains have disappeared, the light is white with snow but the water is still blue. Maldives blue. Dentist-mouthwash blue. Drown-in-your-eyes blue. James is in first. I can see from the thinness of his lips that it is cold, how he is forcing himself to smile and keep going. I lower myself to the stone ledge, hold the rock overhang and the slab underneath me, my legs and arms in the water. I can feel the snow on my bare shoulders, on my chest. My skin is tightening to it. It doesn't feel as cold as rain. Perhaps it is the gentleness of its landing instead of a stiletto-sharp pummelling. There is just a brush, a softness of a crystal wing.

I lower myself slowly, feeling the water reaching my nethers, rising over my stomach. It is so cold it feels scalding. Nerves scream in confusion, saying, whatever it is, you shouldn't be in it. I dive forward and concentrate on my breathing – stretching out in a full stroke towards the end of the pool, where I can see the mountains are now disappearing in snow clouds. I pause at the lip of the pool, where it shelves up and my feet can touch the bottom. The snow is flying fast and if I raise my hand flakes will settle there. I think of the summer when we would lie on the ledge of the weir and see who could get a damselfly to alight on their fingers.

I shout out to James who is already out and drying and notice how my voice has been made strange and hoarse by the cold. I always sing to myself when I swim. It's the way I can tell if I need to get out, the way certain letters get blunted. My 'b's stop working. I turn and swim back again, looking down to the bottom of the pool and think about trying to touch it, imagine how the water would feel around my head, the cold screwing in from the ears, pinching at the bridge of the nose. I picture too how the world would look through the blue lens of the water: the snow falling down towards the surface above me, as if I were driving with it flying at the windscreen. My legs and arms are slowing. The pool is sapping heat from me. It has just been minutes but it's time to get out.

I dress, leaning my back against a rock. My teeth are chattering and I'm struggling to push my numb feet into my socks, but I can't stop grinning, exhilarated by the intensity of the cold water. James is already dressed and standing, looking down at me with Anna. Our voices sound ragged and wild.

Cold weather – the shorthand for that vast spectrum of conditions with the power to transform our world into something glimmering and magical – is generally seen as bad news for our mood and energy levels. The cold can lead to physical lethargy. A lack of sunlight can cause seasonal affective disorder. The human brain can confuse physical responses to chills with interpersonal feelings of coldness. We are more likely to feel listless, dispirited and unhappy in cold weather. Then why am I not feeling that way? Why do I, red of face and cold of toe, enjoy the sensation of drawing in cold air, filling my lungs and, for just a moment, holding a scrap of that winter freeze in my chest? Why do I feel that each time I go into the cold and the ice there is something left in my blood and bones that makes the rest of that day feel more gentle, kinder, happier?

Maybe the answer is because so many of the reports on mood shifts and chemical changes are not actually based on an *experience* of snow, frost, ice or the sensation of super-cooled water on skin. In fact, they are about almost the very opposite. According to *Psychology Today*, cold weather creates stress in the human body not because we are going out, but because we are staying in. Everyday activities are crimped because putting on extra layers is just too much bother. Perhaps it is our unwillingness to go outside in what we consider bad weather that is really damaging our moods.

By the time we are back on the trail, the snow is spreading and the colours of the valley are muted and whitening. The wind here is minimal and the flakes are wet and falling in sticky clumps, rather than being blown to a powder. We are glowing from the cold water and stop to take videos of the snow appearing out of clouds that are now sucking the teeth of Cuillins. Again, I can't get over the flatness of the images, how the camera has failed to capture the differ-ence between the softness and hardness in the landscape. A world of crystals and angles that simultaneously blunts lines and peaks.

The car, when we reach it above the treeline, is mush-roomed in snow that we claw away from the windows. It takes double the time to get back to the cottage. As I drive, I recall the man we had passed on the way to the pools, the one in the bigger car who had wound down his window to tell us it was too treacherous and that we should go back. I slow and then worry that I shouldn't use the brakes. We have stopped talking now. The snow is flying at the windscreen and my knuckles are white on the steering wheel. White and shaped like the Cuillins.

SNOWBALLS. SOUND.
Isle of Skye, December

Driving even short distances on the island is hard work. The roads have to skirt the sharpness of the mountains, the eruptions of rock that swing into view with every turning. The same range from different angles, different distances, but still craggy and sharp despite the snow. Today we are heading to the north-east from the north-west but must first go south and then through a pass in the mountains, which judging from the tyre tracks in the snow has seen only one other vehicle this morning. We drive slowly, the car occasionally flashing up a skid-hazard warning light, the snow coming in fat puffs that melt into tiny wet stars. We had spoken about stopping on the way home to find snow, but now it has come to us. We pull into what looks like a parking area and get out.

The snow sounds so different from the iced-up drifts that we've skittered over in our walks. They had been glassy and crusted as hard as concrete, the edges flint-knapped and glittering. The old flakes crunching under foot like tiny bones. But this fresh fall pillows the foot. It sucks sound away rather than making it.

As soon as the engine stopped, James had leapt from the car behind and within seconds the first snowballs explode on my back. The kids shriek as they are hit too or as they launch their own. We split into gangs, first along family lines and then turn on each other. Snow knocks hats off, lodges in hoods, slithers and droops down collars and backs. I take my gloves off to feel the snow. The cold of its touch is almost like a burning heat, so much so that you can convince your-self that your fingers are warm rather than hurting from pinched veins.

We are by no means quiet, but snow dampens our voices. Snow can absorb up to 60 per cent of sound and our inability to fill the landscape with our clamour makes everything dreamlike. It reminds me of nightmares when I couldn't shout when I needed to, when I couldn't run or walk.

Where we have stopped is not familiar to us, yet there is still a feeling of transformation: the whiteness of the light, the disappearance of fences and roads transports us briefly out of our world. But at the same time, in that act of noticing and feeling, we are more present too.

We are all breathing hard, the endorphins of activity coursing through us. Bending and gathering and ducking and throwing. Under coats and gloves my back and chest are glowing with warmth. I can feel the shine of my face as I can see it on Eliza and Seth, their breath smoking hot. We stop and watch as Lyra makes her escape, galloping up and down a bank and then twisting onto her back, digging her shoulder blades into the fresh fall. She flips, tongue lolling, and commando crawls towards us, leaving a trail of belly-smoothed snow in her wake.

The snow is full of moisture, which means it sticks and holds beautifully. We roll together a base with cartoonish ease, like the sponge of a Swiss roll, cracking but staying firm. James and Seth roll another for the torso and Eliza fashions a head with cat ears and eyes of blue-grey gravel. Jen and Anna, who have been sheltering in the cars taking pictures, get out and we all pose next to the snow cat.

We wrap the dog in a towel and I stand with my hands on Eliza's shoulders. It seems just moments ago that my hands were even smaller than hers are now and had thrown a snowball in an Essex wood, sending it in an impossible arc towards my brother.

Inside the car we turn the heater up. Press our hands between our thighs and wait for the sting of returning sensation. On the radio the news is on. Provisional data (it will later be confirmed) from the Met Office has shown that 2022 is the warmest year on record, with a mean temperature of 10.03°C. The previous all-time high, set in 2014, was 9.88°C. Since 1884, the presenter says, all the ten years recording the highest annual temperature have occurred since 2003. The year will also be the warmest year on record in the 364-year Central England temperature series from 1659, the world's longest instrumental record of temperature.

I wonder how many memories of snow my children will have.

RIME ICE. FREEZING FOG.
Knettishall Heath, January 2023

The cold front is sticking to the east again, like skin against freezing metal. The chill comes back into the house through the floorboards. We use the heating sparingly, shouting at the kids to shut-the-berluddy-door as we try keep heat hostage. My feet are constantly cold. I double sock, then triple sock, until I find it hard to walk up the stairs. The windows of our bedroom are blown and there is a constant mist between the panes. So much so that at first we don't notice the thickness of the fog that has lowered over the roads. It's only when I let the dog out the back and she disappears at the end of the patio that I see its cold, bright whiteness. Out the front, visibility has been reduced to about 50 metres. The church spire has gone, as has the beautician's on the corner.

I still find it hard to not slip into old ways when describing weather. To reach for those tired pathetic fallacies that I discuss with my English classes. To talk of palls and veils, to use words that drip with associations, that have a dirge of greyness to them. Words that suggest the fog is blocking something, obscuring the light rather than creating it. Yet, today, there is a brightness that reminds me of snowfall, when the glare of light on crystal is almost too much, where the eye struggles to find any purchase in the white.

Both snow and fog have the power to wipe out a place completely; its erasure is so absolute, so simple, it can be utterly bewildering, particularly when it happens somewhere you know well. I have felt similar astonishment at death. Like a puzzled dog that doesn't understand television and tries to check the back of the screen to see where everyone has gone. The idea that an entire life can have just disappeared seems impossible.

By the time Jen and I get to Knettishall Heath it is mid-morning and the fog has already lifted, but it has left its mark in the cluster of beech trees by the car park: the leaves that remain on the branch look as if they have been filled with long white pins of rime ice. Even the upper branches, often out of the reach of hoar frost, have grown blackthorn-like defences in the shape of sharp spikes of ice. A white so pure it seems impossible that it has formed naturally from the water of freezing fog, that it hasn't been grown in a lab or printed by polymers.

When we look more closely, angling our camera lenses at it, we can see that some of the bigger spikes have grown other barbs and that the ice is noticeably thicker where the breeze, a gentle south-westerly, has pushed supercooled water droplets into contact with a surface. We measure the spikes with our fingers. One inch. Two inches. On the underside of the same branch, the bark runs smooth and cold. If the fog were still here, rubbing out the landmarks, it would be possible to navigate using the ice, positioning yourself against its sharp fingers to find north.

We walk along the road, over the cattle grid, and then turn off across the heath. The sun is trying to come out, lending a brilliance to the air. A white smokiness that causes the light to bounce wider, longer. We walk along a path that is pine-edged, with the outermost branches rimed; so much so that they look noticeably lower than branches on the other side. The dog is in front, barrelling along in her red coat with a collar that makes her look like a cartoon Dracula. She stops every ten metres to drag her shoulders over some important spot. She always seems to do it in the frost. I wonder if she's trying to get the smell of the cold onto her? Trying to warm up? Get rid of her hated coat? Maybe it is a spot where the Exmoor ponies that graze here spent the night. The paths are indented with their tracks, now frozen as hard as their shoes. It is probable that, like most of the Brecks, this place would have been an open landscape since it was cleared for farming in the Neolithic. But since that time it has always been in the process of becoming or disappearing. Without people to remove them or ponies to graze them, the trees soon move back in, filling in the blanks of the heath. The light and the ice make it easier to see those that have been missed or allowed to grow. Against the bright whiteness of the sky, the iced leaves and branches almost disappear, but the trunks stand as black columns. Line drawings on an empty page.

At the edge of one clearing, some young silver birch have not been beaten back and they are now beautified by ice. The rime has grown to become a fir-tree skin, each thin twig partially wrapped in white needles. We take off our gloves to feel them. I was expecting the ice to be hard, like an icicle, to make a sound when we tap on them. But it is soft and silent. There is no resistance under the finger. It turns to powder. To dust. I try another and another, drawing a line with my finger along the branch, feeling the cold slip in as if the ice hadn't melted at all but had just needled into my skin. I feel slightly embarrassed that I've removed a piece of brightness. That there is now a dark smudge where there was once a miracle of crystals.

Jen points out that since we've got out of the car, we've been almost whispering. She's right. I don't know why, but we still don't raise our voices. There is a glassy quietness

148

to the morning, like water that has gathered its stillness. It is so different from our snowball fight in Scotland. There it felt as if we could shout and never fill the world, but here we speak in hushed tones as if fearful that a raised voice might break something. I worry it would be like the ice that melted beneath my fingertip; once it's gone it will never return. When we hear people nearby calling for their dogs, or just voices in conversation, there's a part of me that shrinks away from the sounds – there's no place for them here. A muntjac barks and breaks cover in a see-sawing, fat-bottomed run. The dog turns and looks at us with her ears up.

We set off again, heading up the heath towards where the trees thicken. The cold seeks out extremities, but this morning it feels as if it has localised around my mouth. It is −3°C but without the wind, there isn't a flaying chill. It is clean. You can feel it move in you, filling the void of your lungs and then steaming back out. There are a few birds around: a green woodpecker the colour of old moss flies away through the pines, thrushes and robins clicking away in the cover, ticking themselves warm. A birch bleached coral white against the darker pines.

We stop at Hut Hill, a bowl barrow that dates from the late Neolithic and stands at Knettishall's highest point. I sat here with Samantha Norris, a good friend who is the ranger here, about four summers ago. She had said she wanted to open up the view from the barrow to the river, that it seemed like something that would be important to the people living here – a view of the river from a place that spoke of life and death, a window between worlds.

We stand at the top and look down a corridor that is bordered by mature silver birch and pines that have spread into fat crowns. The visibility is still poor, but I can make out the dark thread of the Little Ouse, black against the white of fern and heather. A ditch once surrounded the barrow, from where the earth had been taken to bury the bodies, creating the mound that rises above the furze of the heath. Now a woven hedge has filled in its place. One side is woven wood and sprouting branch, the other white and ice-spiked.

Jen is looking for a rose that someone planted years ago, perhaps as a more modern funerary right. It is midday and the sun still hasn't burned through the haze. The fire hasn't taken. I look down to the river, wondering if it has been crusted with ice, and remember reading that icebergs are said to smell like cucumbers. I turn to tell Jen. She is standing looking too, not at the river but where the sun has made the white so bright it almost hurts. Once you've seen it, you can't turn your eyes away. We haw and stamp, send the dog skittering away with a raised arm and a shout. We follow her back through the grove of birch, the ice turning to dust on our coats, the sun still blinking white every time we close our eyes.

As we drive home I realise ice and snow have been a revelation for me. They create landscapes of stillness and serene silence – yet also full of movement and action: creeping frost, thawing ice, falling snow. The crack and crunch of crystal and powder underfoot. Embracing the chill instead of withdrawing from it or bracing myself to face it has transformed the way I experience it. Cold weather demands that we don't sit and wait for it to move around and past us, but that we gladly walk, skate, swim and laugh into the brisk, exhilarating air.

WIND

Perhaps I should have started with wind. After all, it is the driving force behind weather. Wind, at its most simple, is the movement of air between high- and low-pressure systems that themselves are caused by the uneven heating of the earth by the sun. Wind is the world's breath. It is the blood moving under the skin. It is the earth's great equaliser, the air always striving for balance, for equilibrium. If that sounds like poetry as a definition, there is good reason. Because wind is hard to capture and hold down.

Wind is the strangest of weathers. The least tangible, but at the same time the one that seems to have the most obvious impact on how we live. We can't help but feel its invisible force, its great nothingness. It pulls up trees; pushes over walls; carries moisture, heat and pollutants all across the world. The wind has created trade routes and moulded landscapes. And wind has blown throughout this book, bringing rain, snow and ice, gently stirring the fog into existence. Even its absence played a part, marooning us in the doldrums of summer's stagnant heat.* Yet we often underestimate its more subtle power in shaping the world around us. Only when the wind is strong enough to impact on our infrastructure, to throw and smash, do we really pay any attention – and then staying inside is probably the best idea. Its softness, its subtleties, though, go unnoticed. This is what I want to explore, alongside its wildness. And for some reason, just the thought of it makes my heart beat slightly faster.

GUSTS. AEOLIAN SOUND. INVISIBLE FORCES.
Neist Point, December 2022

The roads are winding, spinning to almost nothing as we reach the coast. It's hard to judge wind strength on Skye from sight alone. There are no trees to bend, few chimneys to smoke. But as soon as we park by the cliff edge, it's clear the wind is up. The waterfall is going in the wrong direction. All along the steep step of the cliff that bends away to the east, the runoff from rain and the slow pulses of snowmelt are flung into the air in spindrift fountains. The world bends. The car doors snap like bones being sucked from sockets

---

* The equatorial region of the Atlantic where the trade winds of the two hemispheres meet is called the doldrums. Prevailing winds in the doldrums are very weak and unpredictable, making movement by sail hard to plan.

– and then we are out, feeling the wind push its hands against our chests, throwing sharp salt spit in our faces. It plugs our breath with its own. We gasp then we laugh.

We lean into the wind like children. *Look*, we motion to each other, *we are being supported, we are being carried*. It reminds me of the 'black magic' we were banned from practising in the playground during the last year of primary school. A group of children gathered around another, muttering words: *light as a feather, stiff as a board*. And then a body is held aloft using just one finger each. An impossible weight borne by the smallest of limbs. The gossamer-thin understanding of science, of synchronicity, of bone, muscle and sinew was no match for the thickness, the drooling richness of magic. Now, on the clifftop, the wind is magic too. We are suspended in the air. Leaning. An impossible weight at an impossible angle, held by nothing.

From the edge of the road, looking down, the views are stunning. We look east through spray across Moonen Bay to the cliff head of Waterstein, slumped like the front of an ancient Greek warship. The low glow of a mid-December sun casts a light that itself seems to have been frothed by the wind over the dark curve of the Hoe. The sea is the blue of old ice, set off by the darkness of the basalt rock exposed like gums at the foot of the cliffs. It is hard to gauge from this distance how big the waves are, but the way the spray smokes up from below, as if Skye had been made suddenly volcanic again, hints at a violence. There are clues too in the sound. The wind and the sea are like a jet-engine roar in the shells of our ears.

We pull ourselves away and stagger and laugh along to a path marked by bollards and a cabin, which might once have been – or perhaps will be – a cafe. We take shelter with our backs pressed against its northernmost side and look out at the headland we will walk along. It is huge. Halfway along, dominating it, there is an upstanding crag that reminds me of some giant tanker, its prow raised on the peak of a monstrous wave. This is An t-Aigeach, meaning the Stallion's Head. And it does have a muscular quality to it, a ridge that looks like rippled flesh. Towards it, racing in from the Western Isles, come other horses' heads with white manes of spume. Galloping with the wind at their backs.

The path we want tracks down the headland, but there are other paths too. Slabs that don't seem to lead anywhere. Strange pieces of engineering that are being slowly consumed by grass. Chains and pulleys attached to sunken posts, which clank their way over the cliff head and down to the headland. These are the remains of an aerial ropeway that used to take supplies out to the lighthouse and the keeper's cottages that are still hidden behind the rearing cliff. We walk slowly, pushing almost nervously against the wind. Our hands are busy, trying simultaneously to hold down hoods that are ballooning with cold air, while also gripping onto the handrail, the kids, the dog who has been tethered with a lead should the wind try to play with her like a kite. We take a step at a time. We shout encouragement, exclamations, but the wind takes most of the words, whips them away and hurls them into the sea. Our ears are filled with its noise. The sounds swirl like water.

The wind, on its own, is silent. What we hear is the wind encountering an obstacle, creating what is known as an aeolian sound. Fixed objects such as rocks and buildings and wires cause a constant tone, while moving objects create irregular sounds. The wind helps us hear the very landscape itself.

At the bottom of the steps, the path levels out and from the headland we can see across the Moonen Bay again. The clouds of nimbostratus have been pulled into rags by the wind and in the highest reaches are patches of blue that are only lightly chalked by high cloud. The sea has turned aqua bright against the brown and grey of the cliffs, against the white tips of its own waves. The sea is now all around us. The path is a grey strip that bends around the great basalt jut of An t-Aigeach. There are clutches of hardy people about, holding hats on their heads. One couple, a man and a woman with a sizeable camera, don't look dressed for a December yomp. She poses in front of the snorting sea, rises a shoulder, sets her jaw. Her red hair whips over her face, rising in the air like flames. He takes a picture and another. Got it, he says. They walk further down the path and repeat the photo. The same pose. The same raised outcrop of shoulder.

Eliza and I walk up to a low wall that screens the head-land's northern edge. We press against it, feeling the wind at our back, and look down. The sea is pure churning noise driving into the jagged shoreline, with the wind moving against it, creating shivering semi-circles against the waves. Spume and spindrift are rising everywhere, as if the wind were diving into the water like gannets. At the shoreline the basalt rocks are pure black, their darkness intensified by the shadow of the crag that clashes with the dishrag white of the sky. I lean forward slightly, letting the wind push at my shoulders but then I see Eliza is doing the same and I step back and wrap an arm around her waist. Her hair lashes over her face and she closes her eyes and spreads her arms as wide as they will go. She smiles, a vision of happy wild-ness, as if she were letting the wind run through all of her. I wonder if, like me, she senses the size of the wind, feels it as something bigger than rock and sea, and recognises her own smallness as a result. It's a realisation that brings freedom: life is a tiny, tender, fragile thing, and we should take every chance that comes our way, go wherever opportunity takes us. I hold her tighter. I put my mouth closer to her ear and say, I've got you. I've got you.

In the lee of the crag there is a calmness. A stillness. We gather ourselves and breathe. I can feel my blood fizzing.

All the teachers at my school hate the wind. They say it seems to do something to the kids, to fill them up with energy. To inflate them. Leaving their brains clinking like ships' masts. Research conducted in American schools appears to bear this out. During one study, when the wind speed was above force 6 (large branches in motion, whistling heard in telegraph wires, umbrellas used with difficulty), the number of playground fights doubled. Another study, this time examining physical fitness at different temperatures, found peak efficiency was at force 4 (raises dust and loose paper, small branches moved).

Physiologically, there is evidence that the wind changes us. Adrenalin production increases. Metabolism speeds up. The blood vessels of the heart dilate, increasing blood flow and the availability of oxygen. Pupils widen. The skin contracts, forcing hairs to stand on end. The body prepares for fight or flight.

It is not clear why humans are so sensitive to wind. Perhaps it is an evolutionary throwback: a state of high alert created by conditions that mask the approach of predators, cause threats to shelter, or to life and limb. What we do know is that staying in the wind maintains that state of emergency. The heart keeps pumping, harder and harder. Our nervous system groans under the pressure, under the stress. Yet, to us, it might not seem like stress at all. Lyall Watson, writing in *Heaven's Breath: A Natural History of Wind*, says that the feeling, to begin with at least, 'may amount almost to euphoria'. It is a sensation that the geographer Ellsworth Huntington said motivated a small, 'usually very quiet' boy,

who he watched 'climb to the top of a tall tree when a violent wind came up, and swing in the branches, singing at
the top of his voice'.[1] Some suggest that it was a reaction
to the constant stimulation of the sharav wind (the name
for the easterly wind that brings warm air from the Arabian
peninsula and the Sahara) that led Bishop James Pike to
walk to his death in the desert near the Dead Sea in 1969.
And while those of us who live and work in the wind may
become used to the stress of it, for anyone unused to being
exposed to weather, it can all get a bit much (even if we
stay at home). Heart attacks and strokes are both thought
to be more common on windy days. Researchers from Lund
University in Sweden cross-referenced 274,000 heart-attack
patients with the weather on the day they were admitted
to hospital between 1998 and 2013. They found that when
the wind speed reached force 7 the number of heart attacks
rose by 7 per cent.[2]

Some research has shown that exposure to the sharav
changes the amount of hormones in our body. The phar-
macologist Felix Sulman reported that around one third of
the Israeli population claimed they had a negative reaction
to the wind.[3] Of these, 43 per cent were found to have an
unusually high concentration of serotonin in their urine.
Serotonin, which controls constriction of blood vessels and
controls sleep and mood development, is a natural tranquil-
liser. But, as Watson says, 'too much of it produces clinical
symptoms which include migraines, allergic reactions,

flushes, palpitation, irritability, sleeplessness and nausea'.[4] The same study found that a further 44 per cent of 'wind casualties' were found to have no adrenalin in their urine, resulting in apathy and depression.

The UK only has one named wind: the Helm. That too is connected with unpleasantness. The mountaineer and author Claude E. Benson, writing in the Yorkshire Ramblers' Club's 1911 journal, described it as a 'mad, boisterous, head-long, bullying wind' that 'chills you to the marrow, crams your hat over your eyes, blows your umbrella not inside out but down on the stick, and ends up by bashing you down with inconsiderate violence upon Mother Earth'.[5] Its ferocity has even been attributed to the supernatural. According to some, the modern name of Cross Fell – where the Helm wind dwells – dates from the erection of a cross at the summit to drain the wind's demonic power. No holy intervention has yet managed to tame it.

The Helm isn't the only wind to be seen as ungodly. In Argentina, the dust-filled Zonda is known as the 'witches' wind' because of the sleeplessness and depression it inflicts. The same name has been given to the Foehn (*föhn*) – a warm, dry downslope wind – in Leukerbad, Switzerland, which some residents say they know has arrived any time the sirens of the emergency services begin in earnest.[6] Then in North America there is the 'devil's wind' of Santa Ana that flattens buildings and has been linked with an increase of murders in Los Angeles county.

All across the world, where there is wind, there is unease and strangeness. Moodiness, malady and madness.

James and Seth are still playing in the wind. We left them jumping from a concrete platform that formed another part of the old aerial rope – the lighthouse delivery system. Anna points out to sea, where the horizon has hazed. She is a farmer's daughter, raised on weather. Looks like rain, she says. Out there it is already raining. Soon the wind will bring it to us. Driven by gusts like this, the rain will feel like cut glass on our skin. It will be hard even to keep our eyes open.

As soon as James and Seth reach us, we push on round the corner, squinting into the wind that rushes into our faces. We are lower now, looking to the south again, and the sea is booming, jackhammer loud. It bellyflops against rocks. I can see the size of the waves. What looked like ripples and gentle movement from the clifftop is a rolling swell. Sharp-edged and explosive. There is still blue above the Hoe, but the bare rock of its upper heights is in shadow from smoky puffs of cloud. There is a well-trodden route to the top of An t-Aigeach, but the wind is too strong and the light too fleeting. We stay on the path curving around the outcrop until the lighthouse comes into view, crouched on the exposed rock. If we're going to reach it before the rain arrives, we need to move quickly, to follow the path of telegraph poles that stand drunkenly alongside the path. But our heads are everywhere, the chaos of the wind rubbing off on us.

We clamber up rocks to take photos of each other goon-ing around, leaning into the wind, standing on rocks with our arms wide, as if we are on the prow of a ship rather than this prow of rock. We take videos of the crash and thunder of the sea, recordings filled with light and move-ment and a black roar that sounds like rocks being ground between teeth. A constant, endless explosion. It reminds us of the podcasts we've been listening to on the way up. Dramatisations of famous hauntings, modern accounts of things that are ghostly and strange. Recordings of nothing that, when listened to more closely, seem to contain a voice. The wind that is constantly in our ears has been given a new intensity, a volume and a coarseness that is shocking. A low, grumbled word.

From a distance the lighthouse looks as if it is rusting. But up close you can see that it and the keeper's cottages are white, with the detailing completed in a sandy-coloured paint. It reminds me of the thick custard of school dinners. It picks out bricks around the three windows on the tower. The main gallery, the walls of the service room, are the same colour. Against that, white railings and a white metal ladder lead up to the lantern-room gallery where the lens is kept. A huge, peeled glass eye, cross-hatched with black metal astragals that cut the glass into triangles. On top of it all is a black bail vent and a weathervane shaped like an arrow. Its flights are held by the westerly wind. I wonder what it would be like to stand here on watch in a storm.

Lighthouses are strange places. Places that tell people to stay away rather than to draw near. Not buildings of heart and family but of isolated foreboding. Even here, a land lighthouse, rather than a marooned stack, the cottages and tower are cut off from the island by a wave of rock. It is tied in place by pulleys and winches. Standing 19 metres high, 43 metres above sea level, the light from the tower is equivalent to 480,000 candles and can be seen up to 38 kilometres away. Built in 1909 (the foghorn, which no longer works, was completed a year later), the lighthouse has been operated remotely by the Northern Lighthouse Board since 1990.

We walk around the low wall and I think about how much care has gone into preserving this building, protecting it from the salt and spray and wind. Part of me wants to get inside, to see if there are still waterproofs hung there like old skins. To see if the cupboards still contain the tins and bottles that were winched down over the rocks, swinging in the wind. I wonder if there are mugs lined up by the taps, if the clock on the wall is still ticking down to the next watch.

Maybe it is the squatness of the cottages or the violence of the wind but I think again of school. The previous week I had taught Seamus Heaney's 'Storm on the Island' to my Year 11 GCSE class. It's a monologue told from the perspective of an islander facing up to the extremes of weather. Yes, there are other meanings too: it is an allegory for the Troubles; the word Stormont is locked inside the title like an ammonite in a rock. But it was the weather that the pupils seized on. They chewed over the pregnant last lines that describe the aggressor as nothing but air and seemed both fascinated and confused by the idea. They talked of thin air being made thick, how wind is a dark matter that is invisible apart from its effects on other things. The wind is a nothing that can unpick the burrowing roots of trees; a nothing that can push fences and levitate trampolines; a nothing that can bow our backs. It is a force that can wobble the solidity of our everyday. It is godlike. It is magic.

In her book *Weatherland*, Alexandra Harris describes how meteorological phenomena, including wind, are 'serially elusive'; as hard to pin down and as changeable as the thoughts and feelings that they have come to represent. Warmth and cold, like the wind, are both felt and not touched. They, as in Heaney's poem, are 'huge nothings'. But I can't help thinking that this doesn't accurately capture our experience of weather. In the West, where our environment is conceived of as either material or immaterial, there is no space left for any phenomena that fall into both categories: sometimes tangible earth, sometimes ephemeral sky.

The anthropologist Tim Ingold, taking his lead from the phenomenologist Maurice Merleau-Ponty, suggests that weather should be thought of in the same way as light. Merleau-Ponty famously claimed our ability to see objects in the environment was in many ways unremarkable. Yet, he went on, the fact we can see at all is almost beyond belief. This sight is made possible by light and every time we experience light we have an experience of being. As William James said, 'The first time we see light . . . we are it rather than see it.'[7]

Building on this idea, Ingold suggests that weather is, in the same way, an experience of light. It is an experience of being. We feel it with every sense. We live, he argues, in a 'weather-world', where earth and sky are linked within one indivisible field and where humans 'make their way through a world-in-becoming' rather than some preformed, static surface. Our world is forever dynamic, 'always unfolding, ever changing in its moods, currents, qualities of light and shade, and colours, alternately damp or dry, warm or cold, and so on'.[8]

Weather then, is not something that happens to the landscape or something that happens to us; it is a way of experiencing the world. It is the light with which we see. We are, as humans, *in* weather. No, more than that. We *are* weather.

And outside, standing on a rock, with the wind rushing over us, it is impossible not to feel part of it all.

As the skies continue to darken, the dog is the first to decide it's time to turn back. She employs a tactic of running at full speed forward, only to turn and dash back in the opposite direction to get maximum arm crack on the lead. Maybe she can smell the rain, can sense a change in pressure, or maybe she's just tired of the wind. I think we're all flagging a little. I find myself leaning into gusts then staggering forward when they disappear. Like when my brother used to hold me away with a long arm as I swung angry pre-teen punches, only to fall when he sidestepped. I don't know if it's the physicality or if it's the over-stimulation, but Eliza is exhausted. I lift her onto my back and I walk on, her head on my shoulder, her mouth near my ear. Her breath audible over the wind. The rain overtakes us as we climb the steps back towards the car park.

In the car, the silence is audible. Our ears ring with it. Our voices seem too loud, too crashing for a small space. I think of nights spent lying in darkness after shouting in clubs and pubs. The blood still hammering. The car rocks gently to the strongest gusts, fills wheel arches and pushes at windows. The spray is still being driven vertically upwards. Above the cliff, above the spume, above the salt, a hooded crow slides sideways. It looks like a film clip being rewound.

OLD WINDS. OLD WAVES. SLEET BOW.
Isle of Skye, December 2022

It is early afternoon and the wind is up and scorching cold. Blowing hard from the north. We meet it head on at An Corran beach, at the far tip of Skye. The clouds are thick and yellowing in a way that looks as if more snow is on the way. But to the south-east the clouds have been pushed away to reveal distant mountains that are perhaps on Rona, perhaps on the mainland. They look like a vision of some heavenly land. Something from a fairy tale. They float impossibly above a sea the colour of flint, sandwiched in clouds. The peaks are bathed in light and they glow as if they were veined with gold. To the north, a stretch of black sand has been revealed, but it is the newly exposed rocks we head for. Big black boulders, cracked with stones jammed in. Weed-slimed pavements of mudstone that still hold a salty skim of water.

The temperature has dropped with the direction of the wind and the tracks around the cottage have become perilous to run on. The puddles are frozen solid and patterned with white rings. On the beach it feels as if there is ice too in the sea spray, that the rocks that we slip and lurch over are slicked with more than just water. The wind is a hand at our back. But we need to go slowly anyway to find what we're looking for. I watch the dog skitter from rock to rock, attempting to keep her belly out of the water, and then I look back down. The wind creates patterns on the deeper pools. It looks as if someone has blown on it or something small is swimming under the surface.

There is movement in the pooled water, but there is also movement in the rock. Or at least there was. Below the dark shadows of ripples, the yellowish stone holds ridges and lines, hints of whorls. I dip a hand beneath the pools and feel the trackways of old flows. Old tides. Fingerprints of both ancient water and ancient weather: the wind-pushed, wave-sculpted patterns left in the sand, frozen for millions of years. According to researchers at MIT, certain patterns – whether modern or prehistoric – can give us clues about the conditions: hourglasses, zigzags or tuning forks suggest times of storms and points of environmental flux. We are lucky to see these ones. In summer they are often buried. Today the wind and the fierceness of the sea has exposed them, scouring them clean of sand. But the rocks here don't just contain ripples.

James and Seth are shouting at us, waving us over. Their words jut through the gaps in the wind and the crashing hiss of the breakers. At first glance, it's hard to see what they are pointing at. Partly because of the seaweed that softens the edges, and the fact that it is under a few inches of shimmering water. But also, it is just so big. The brain can't slot it into our modern schemas. It says, no, it can't be a footprint. Seth holds a splayed hand above it, then uses his foot to dangle it above each of the three toes. The reflection of the dog's face, peering down, fills up just a heel. And there are more. Once you find one, you can't help but find others. All across the rock, right up to the lip of the sea that roars with the wind, dark depressions filled with water, with stones, with fringes of bright green weed, evolve into a tridactyl of three splayed toes, each one as big as a brick, shaped like arrowheads. They remind me of cat prints, pressed into wet cement.

This fossilised trackway, or ichnite, was made by dinosaurs around 165 million years ago in sand or mud around a shallow, warm sea. Almost 100 million years before the gabbro rocks of the Cuillin were formed. It is thought that they were most likely created by a group of Megalosaurus, a carnivore that walked on two legs and measured around 10 metres in length.

It is a strange feeling to touch them. To be connected in some way with the movements of something so old and alien. I kneel down and float my hand above it, trying to imagine the water is blood warm, that the wind is not knifing and cold.

We leave the rocks and walk north across sand that is black and sticky. James says it reminds him of Iceland. The volcanic beaches, the air that tastes like iron. The dog shuttles between us as we let the wind rattle our heads. Lyra is playing her own game. She moves in frantic circles, running grooves into the sand. She does it with an urgency, as if she is trying to convey a message. A circle. Stops, panting. Drops down on her haunches, her long tongue lolling and spoon-like, speckled with white spit and black sand. Then up again. Another circle. Repeat.

The light is changing on the beach. The brightness that framed the mountains when we arrived has spread across the sky. The water has turned from flint to become that old ice blue. A colour of tropical warmth that spits sleet and a blistering chill onto a volcanic dark beach. Out above Staffin Island there is a rainbow in the sky. A yellowing, bruise-like sleetbow.

In the shallows, the peak of the Quiraing, the northernmost summit of the Trotternish ridge, is reflected in the sand. Puddled and snow-dripped. Seth has borrowed Jen's camera and stands on rocks and tries to capture the light. The spray rises around his silhouetted shape. He returns, huffing, his cheeks red despite the pinched hood of his parka. He's frustrated the camera hasn't caught what he saw. He shows me the back of the camera and then nods towards the brittle light that frames the rounded folds of the peak. He shouts over the wind that he's going to try again, to capture it before it goes. I put a hand on his shoulder. Sometimes noticing in the moment can be enough.

NAMED STORMS. WIND GODS. WHISPERING LEAVES.
Wrabness, February

Today will see the first named storm of 2023 hit the UK. A low-pressure system that is predicted to bring rain and high winds across the country. According to the weather maps and forecasts, the winds will be strongest in the north: in the Hebrides, around mainland Scotland and the north-east of England. A big swell is predicted for the North Sea: force 9 on the Beaufort scale (wave crests topple over and spray affects visibility) to force 10 (sea surface largely white). Although the east will not see the strongest winds, the wind-finder app that I use on my phone shows three large arrows following the river valley as it opens up into the sheltered waters at the rump of East Anglia.

Humans have a long history of naming weather, for ascribing intention and personality, especially when it involves wind. The power and ephemerality of wind has meant that many of the names are also associated with divine powers. Certainly, for the ancient Greeks, the wind and the gods were indivisible. On the Tower of Winds in Athens, an octagonal monument to the wind and thought to be the world's first meteorological station (it features sundials, a water clock and a wind vane), each of the eight sides is adorned with a carving of a different wind represented as a winged man. A whole compass of personalities, from cloud-shrouded Euros in the east to Zephyros the gentle messenger of spring in the west. On the north-facing side hovers Boreas, the bringer of winter, whose voice is amplified to a shriek through a conch shell.

While the spread of Christianity might have seen the winds partially stripped of their identity as deities, they were still seen as an extension of God, carrying holy messages. The scattering of the Spanish Armada by an Atlantic storm was not coincidental, not just good chance, but a Protestant wind. A caricature of it appeared on coins and provided a divine seal of approval for the Reformation. The weather during the Civil War was also thought to be partisan. The death of Oliver Cromwell in 1658 was preceded by a sizeable storm that became known as Oliver's Wind. While some claimed it as the sky's great gnashing and wailing at the Lord Protector's demise, others suggested the strong winds were demons coming to claim one of their own.

Assigning names helped winds be understood and seen. Names are clothing, a dust to be blown onto the invisible man. Meteorologists in the USA began to realise in the 1950s that giving storms names could help to increase awareness about the potential impacts of extreme weather – especially if two storms were swirling across the landmass at the same time. At first the National Hurricane Center used only women's names to communicate details about tropical cyclones but in 1979 they began alternating with men. The move, which seemed uncontroversial enough, has since been blamed for a rise in fatalities and an increase in wind-related damage. A study in 2014 by scientists at

Princeton University[9] suggested that storms with typically female names caused 'significantly more deaths' as they were viewed as being less threatening and therefore less of a risk. In other words, people are more likely to prepare for storm Mark than storm Margaret.

It wasn't until 2015 that the UK's Met Office and the Met Éireann also decided to start naming storms, affixing monikers to any system with the potential to prompt an amber or red weather warning. The launch of the system in 2015, which included an appeal for name suggestions, was again about raising public awareness. A Met Office spokeswoman said that people had an affinity for the names, they 'latched' on to them. Spread across social media, they helped create awareness among groups that were 'harder to reach'. In 2019, the Royal Netherlands Meteorological Institute (KNMI) joined the initiative in recognition that storms and winds were living, migrating forces that didn't respect borders. Tracking a storm across sea and land when it has a single name would be easier.

The public still gets to choose the names of storms. Each year, the three organisations ask for suggestions and the names are cued up ready and waiting for the wind to take them. They are ordered alphabetically, alternating gender, from A to Z – although storms have yet to get past the letter K (Storm Katie blew out in 2016).

I like the naming of storms. I don't know why. Part of it is the personification, the fact the winds still have godlike power. It's just that their names are more likely to be Bertie or Darren. This storm, as the first of the year, should begin with an A. The name Antoni is ready to be taken. After that comes Betty, Cillian, Daisy, Elliot, Fleur and Glen. But in fact it was christened Otto by the Danish Meteorological Society who tracked it unspooling across the Atlantic. I think I'm glad the Danish got there first. To me Antoni suggests unseasonal heat. A short, hot temper. I picture Otto as blond and unhurried, his breath as cool as ice.

Eliza is shouting up at me to come down. Telling me to be careful. She's using her serious voice now. Newly learned. The same one she uses to admonish me for standing on the very top of the stepladder to get into the loft, to tell me it's not designed for that. She sighs. Throws her hands up in exasperation, looks to her brother who is poking mud with a stick and then to my dad who is taking pictures with his camera and muttering dark warnings about fire engines and their ability to access remote locations. I tell her not to worry, that I'll just be one second and, yes, I promise I'll be careful. She clings to the bottom of the trunk and squints up.

The tree had been easy to climb. The oak's trunk was slanted so it was almost possible to run up the first few feet, before using lower branches, many of which were barkless and creaking, to pull myself up into the V of the fork. I stand there now, a foot braced in that angle between boughs where a squirrel has dropped an autumn's split acorns. I loop my arms around a branch that is thigh thick and scramble up until I am standing almost in the tree's crown, looking through branches that sway drunkenly over the muddy beach of the Stour estuary. Below is a thick bank of reeds, yellow as ripe wheat, beyond that saltmarsh. Full of burrows and footprints. In the distance I can see the tide has thinned the river to a gasp of cold blue water.

Standing in the tree I can see and feel the wind. The gusts that had hit us as we entered the valley and stood on the green slope down to the broad estuary of the Stour are still moving around me, running over the river. The thinnest outermost branches of the oak are dark and dusted with lichens the colour of mustard powder and blackboard chalks. When the hardest gusts come, the tree stretches like a bow and the twigs rattle like old bones. The neighbouring trees grind in response. Bark against bark.

One of my friends climbs trees regularly. She often talks about the sounds of trees, or rather the sounds that come from the vibration of leaf and bough. The sound of wind through trees is called psithurism, from the Greek *psíthyros*, meaning 'whispering'. The founder of the RSPB, W. H. Hudson, thought the sound of the wind in trees was 'restorative'[10] and would happily spend an hour listening to the movement above him. Perhaps the power of the wind to create stress is tempered when it is filtered through the limbs of the tree.

Naturalist John Muir certainly never appeared to see the wind in the trees as anything other than positive. He described how each tree reacted to the wind differently; each sang its 'own song' and made its own 'peculiar gestures'. For him, it was the pine that was his favourite tree to experience in the wind. 'They are,' he said, 'mighty waving golden-rods, ever in tune, singing and writing wind music all their long century lives.'[11]

In my tree, there are no leaves to whisper, but the wood itself hums with movement. The fibres of the trunk tense and relax as the wind sweeps along the estuary. A tremble that doesn't so much come through the skin but vibrates more deeply. It is a bass note. A nasal hum. I think of the poplar tree on the bank of the Little Ouse where I often go to swim. In February I had gone during a window between storms Dudley and Eunice to find the tree had been toppled; unseamed, from the knave to the chaps. The break is not where you'd have expected it to be: close to the ground where the wind tests the trunk's strength like fingers on an asparagus spear. It was more than halfway up. The stump, the shard, that remained was angular and toothy. All exposed pale heart and twisted fibres. It looked like a fresh artillery strike. An explosion. An act of violence that left the uppermost branches, the leafless crown, lying almost completely across the river's flow, the water bunched behind it like a heavy skirt. I imagine what that would have sounded like when it went down. The sharp crack, snap, tear of it.

The wind is ringing in my ears now and I have to remind myself again that I am not hearing the wind but the things that the wind touches. I wonder whether I am hearing the sound of my own ears, whether my whole body is vibrating like the heartwood of a tree and at the centre of it all are those tiny bones in my ear.

All wind is air in motion, travelling between areas of different pressure. When the weather is warm, air will rise, creating areas of low pressure; when it is cool, air descends, making areas of high pressure. But nature is about balance. If two neighbouring areas of air are at different pressures in the atmosphere, they will equalise: air is forced from high pressure to low pressure. The movement, the sucking of air, which we experience as a cracked-cheek blow, is wind. And this wind, unlike small-scale winds such as sea breezes, has travelled. It has crossed sea and land. It has touched countless trees; it has vibrated the bones of God knows how many people. How far has this wind come to reach me? I close my eyes and just feel the movement of the tree, the movement of the wind. I wrap my arms tighter, pull my cheek close to the roughness of the bark; this is what it's like to realise you are not in control. The wind *hmmmnnns* again and the tree shakes it off, from its heartwood to the mad scribble of its twigs.

I climb down and we set off again. Eliza loops her arm through mine, while my dad and Seth lope on ahead to catch up with Jen and my mum. It is sheltered behind the trees and the bank, and I miss the feel of the wind. As the others stick to the path that leads up through woodland, I pull Eliza to one side and we scramble over tree roots and slip down onto the estuary beach. The Stour is darker under the clouds. A naval grey. The mud is a sandy red that, closer to the water, is being picked apart by waders. Their prints are lopsided stars on a surface that is littered with white clam shells the size of thumbnails. Seaweed is piled into greasy molehills and the air tastes of salt and iodine.

We stop by an oak that is below the tide line. It has been stripped of bark and the wood itself is deeply scored. Some of the grooves are inches deep and full of small stones. I wonder if it is the stones that have caused the patterns on the tree. It is almost as if the bark has been drawn back on. Next to the tree is part of a pipe, its main body rusted to almost nothing, but the thicker metal of its openings is still intact and proud of the mud. We put our fingers through the rivet holes and pinch nostrils at the stink of the gut weed.

A curlew calls and we stand back up to look for them. There are redshank. Brent geese with sooty black heads. Dunlin, far away by the waterline, rise in clouds; first brown then the white of their bellies as they turn, the brightness flashing like a smile.

My dad phones when we return to the trail. He wants to know if we are far away. If we know where we are going. We hurry to meet them, huffing up the muddy path to find them talking to two men who have been foraging. One of them, wearing a tweed cap and smoothing down a rollie with his thumbs, nods to a tea towel full of oyster mushrooms with bright white gills and tops the colour of clotted cream. He says that these would have been triggered into growth by the cold snap. The streets of altostratus that stretch out over the valley signal that warm weather is now on its way. This winter has careered from mild to deep freeze and back again.

The ancient Greeks placed wind at the start of time. The dancing of a naked Eurynome moved the air and created the North Wind, which in turn became the serpent Ophion. The coming together of the pair resulted in the laying of an egg from which all life hatched. Writer Nick Hunt notices that wind and life are yoked by language.[12] The words 'wind', 'breath' and 'spirit' are one and the same in Hebrew (*ruach*) and Arabic (*ruh*). The Greek word for wind, *aenmos*, is the root word of the Latin *anima*, meaning 'soul': the force that animates. The Latin word *spirare*, which means breathe or blow, is the root of spirit and respiration. Breeze, a word that has now been shorn of its definite sea-going meanings, was known by the Greeks as the *zoogo-noi*, meaning 'life-begetters'.

Modern meteorology was born through the wind. Today's forecasts are the breezy offspring of wind maps – the drawing of wind patterns to predict future weather events. While it would take modern technology – computers, satellites – to give us the accuracy we currently enjoy, even in the late eighteenth century there were breakthroughs in understanding the importance of wind. In 1777, the physician Erasmus Darwin, grandfather of Charles – who rigged a weathercock to a dial in his study – noticed that 'the change in the direction of the wind evidently changes its tendency to absorb or give out heat'. His conclusion that there were different 'districts of air' that met with others of different qualities and temperatures is the frontrunner of the Frontal theory that emerged in the 1920s. Although he described the theory of the wind as being 'imperfect' he recognised that if it was successfully contemplated in the future, 'the produce and comfort of this part of the world would be doubled at least'.

In December, I visited Cambridge's Botanic Garden to record the weather, to see the theory in action. Weather stations are scattered all across the UK. Along with the Met Office's network of 200 automated weather stations that measure air temperature; atmospheric pressure; rainfall; wind speed and direction; humidity; cloud height and visibility, there are many other partially automated sites and manual sites that also send data to the Weather Observations Website (known by its rather excitable acronym of WOW). Weather stations are all different, by virtue of their location, their siting in topography, but the same in the type of measurements taken and often the kit used. All are designed to turn the weather into codes. To translate experience into something that can be counted, compared and stored.

The temperature had changed dramatically overnight. Although there were still a few piles of snow – places where it was piled to keep paths clear – the ground was thawing. When I walked around the fenced perimeters, I could see the ice in the brook and in the ponds was breaking up. Surfaces that just days ago were thick enough to walk on had dwindled to thin panes, like old glass. There was a dampness to the garden. A deep, dark smell of newly uncovered earth and mulch.

And sure enough, when we recorded the wind direction, noting the curl of steam from the heating system, we could see the wind direction had changed. The northerlies that had locked in the cold had been replaced by a south-westerly that ushered in a milder clime.

We drive back down to Manningtree for lunch and walk on the small beach behind the pub. Everyone is in good spirits. There is a lightness to everything. Outside the cloud has been pushed back, broken up to form a grey strip of alto-cumulus that sits in a largely blue sky. A metal barrier that sits across the back of the pub garden vibrates in the breeze.

Back home Jen shares photos and videos of the day. There is Eliza after she walked off the estuary quay think-ing the mud was sand. There are her boots that have been turned to blocks of ooze. There the flat surface of the estu-ary pitted where Seth had dug out the boots with his hands after Eliza had extracted herself. Videos of the sound of the wind, big and crashing, full of drama like an iceberg carving. The sea raging around it as well. All of the videos have voices in them. Eliza whistling. My mum making a strange *ooh oohing* noise to the dog. Jen's tired voice saying, yes, you're in this one as well.

The wind keeps rattling at the microphone. Shouting like a lost ghost.

RABBITS. KITE FLYING.
Suffolk, March

The rabbit looks as if it is in the process of being unwrapped. The feet are wearing fur boots, but the bones of the legs have popped out of the seams and are crossed neatly at the knee. The bone is the same soft grey as the sky. It is hard to make out many other features. I think I can see the shape of an ear, a dandelion puff of scut, but the rest of the body is just an empty rag looped over a branch; a puppet waiting for a hand. We wonder how it got there; eight or nine feet up an oak tree, a place where a rabbit – alive or dead – has no real business being. The wind gusts again and the movement of the wind in the tree makes the feet wag like fingers from side to side. I think it's probably what caught our attention in the first place. An unexpected jiggle in an unexpected place. Jen has walked on, nervous that Lyra will disappear into one of the hundreds of rabbit holes underneath the blackthorn if she stands still too long. She calls over from further down the track; she's standing on tiptoe, peering at something. Shouting to be heard over a mild wind that is clicking branches together.

'There's another one here. Look. And another one!'

It's the cusp between winter and spring. The weather doesn't seem to be shifting softly but see-sawing between freezing and unseasonably mild. In conversational parlance, it can't make up its mind. For the past two days the north wind has ushered in air that burns with Arctic cold: the streets smell of wood smoke; the car windscreens are feathered with ice. Then, this morning, a south-westerly pushed back, rattling at the windows, blowing a low drone down the side of the house and over the chimney. The semi-circles, at least in the south and the east, took the triangles. Ground has been gained.

I worked downstairs and Jen upstairs in an attempt not to distract each other, but we both struggled to get anything done. I felt washed out. Drained. Jen says maybe it's because we worked over the weekend, or maybe it's because of the change in pressure. When she comes down early in the afternoon and finds me staring out of the window, watching the lash of the trees at the end of the garden and the ivy that grows in a ball on our garden fence fill with sparrows, she suggests a walk. She has, she says, a window. No meetings until four and we both need to blow the cobwebs away. I love the expression. The idea that we have become so sedentary, so still and housebound that we have been dressed in spider silk. But I also liked the idea of letting the wind in.

In Anglo-Saxon times, a window was an *eagperl*, an eyehole. They were places in buildings where you could look out, to locate threats, to check on livestock and weather. When the Norse arrived – travelling 320 kilometres in a day, if the winds were right – it was their word, *vindauga*, meaning 'wind eye', that took over. Glass would have been rare then; confined to only the most important buildings. The openings of most houses would be only loosely covered, maybe with hides or skins. It made sense that windows became known for what they let in. It feels as though I have let something in with the weather. I'm yearning to let it in again.

And so now we are near the top of Hartest Hill – part of the Newmarket Ridge – a place we chose as being close by and relatively exposed, looking at the remains of rabbits that have been scattered in the tops of trees and hedges. Some are just hindquarters, one a sharp-spurred spine. We stand on the mud path that sweeps down the hill. On the right thick hedges, on the left a field that is still lined from the seed drill. Above us is the latest find, the freshest yet, reclining on its back on the very top of the bramble bush. It looks as if it parachuted in. They all do. Through the hedge I can see the field drops steeply down to a small copse and how the whole bank is pitted with entrances to a warren. A buck runs from one patch of bramble to another, ears up, eyes wide, its whole body stretched with the need for survival. Lyra lets out a low rumbling growl.

We wonder what could have happened. One? Maybe a dog walker slung it out of the way. But four or five? Jen says that when she was at a rural college there used to be parties in the woods, held by some of the well-heeled undergraduates. She said they were particular about who came. Invite only. Apparently anyone trying to find it without instructions would find things hanging in the dark. Dead, wet things. Skinless things that had been butchered and turned inside out.

There is the sound of an aeroplane above the movement of the wind in the trees and the hedges. A few cut-glass syllables from a skylark and then a different call. Not a buzzard's mew but the kind of noise young children make when they are pretending to whistle but scream instead. A shrieking *weeoo-weeoo-weeoo* that enters the ears hot and stays there, as if something has broken off inside. The bird is too high to see in any detail and it looks as though it is still going up, as if it has been caught on a tide and is being drawn out. It is too far away for me to see the reddish-brown of its body, the white of its tail and the hands of the black-tipped wing. Even with our hands shielding our eyes against the brightness of this grey afternoon, it's hard to see much more than a silhouette. But what else do you really need? The angled wings, the deep notch of that forked tail. The way it moves as if it is pulled by strings. The brain colours in the rest. Red kite.

I always thought that the kite was named after the toy. That the way it moves as if its tail had been pulled by strings to respond to the gusts meant the name was carefully chosen. But in fact, it's the other way around. The word kite is likely derived from the Old English *cȳta* and related to the German for screech owl. The bird is named for its noise, the toy for the way it seems to share the movements of the hovering bird.

When I was young we had a kite with a kite on it. At least that's what I said. My brother just said hawk or eagle. But in my mind when I think back to that stunt kite, thin white plastic stretched over flimsy plastic spars, it was definitely a kite. The red chest, the grey head, the yellow eye. Our kite was only ever flown on holiday. Occasionally on the beach, or more often on the cliffs or promenade above, where the wind was stronger (there's less frictional resistance higher up, allowing the kite to pick up speed). My dad would run with it, before throwing it into the air, while my brother – it was his kite, a birthday present from a friend – pulled on two green handles.

Most of the time the flights were brief. The kite went up, turned and dived into the ground. But sometimes, I guess when the wind caught it in just the right way, when my dad's throws went that bit higher, it stayed suspended there in the air, the plastic snickering. Then I would sit and watch, begging for a loop-the-loop, for the strings to be fed out. To be allowed to have a go and let it go higher. Higher. Please. Please. My brother would stand grim-faced with concentration and I would sit, head snapped back, watching this thing become something else. Giving him a taste of the wind. One holiday I followed its flight so intently that I toppled backwards from the steel bar I was sitting on and cracked my head open on the concrete.

Perhaps in the same holiday, or at least a long time ago as the memory feels strange and old when I reach for it, I was taken to see the kites feeding. Real kites. We were standing a distance away, again on a hill I think, while meat was tossed into the field. The air, thick and cloying, smelling like a butcher's shop, had become black with birds. In fact, I don't remember noticing a single individual bird. They were a sense of movement. Angles and shapes. A swirling gas. A force that snatched up meat and dropped it again. I recall a faint horror too. The same feeling I had when I saw a raven at the Tower of London. Its unpeeled eye staring at me while it swallowed down red cubes of beef.

The kite is a bird associated with greed, with scavenging, with death – the collective noun for kites is a wake. During the early modern age, when Shakespeare was writing and when the bird was still common, the kite was known as a puttock, a word that also came to be used as an insult. Perhaps we are uncomfortable with something that seems so fond of death.

The kite we saw first flies lower. I can see the forked tail being pulled. The twist of it reminds me of a skateboarder in mid-jump; that moment when forward motion has stopped but gravity has yet to claim its own. The bird calls and dips behind one of the scrubby hedges and almost immediately two more rise in its place. One is noticeably bigger. As with most raptors, there is sexual dimorphism in kites. The larger bird is likely a female, although it would take a blood test to tell for sure. She tracks slowly across the field, while the male faces into the breeze and hovers. It is impressive.

I can't recall who, but one of my friends (it might even have been Jen) once said they understand the science of flying, but they don't believe it. The idea that a plane, a heavy metal machine full of people, can somehow stay aloft, is ridiculous. Seeing a kite hover, I have a similar feeling of incredulity. I know that, like a kestrel – once known as the windhover or the windfucker – they face into the wind and flutter their wings and use their tails to hold their position. They fly at a speed that is equal to the wind. Like one of those swimming pools where you swim against jets of water. But the kites seem too large to pull it off. I'm almost waiting for this stunt kite to nosedive into the earth. I wonder what it must feel like to be held by the wind like that, whether the bird feels the same euphoria that we did on top of that rocky outcrop on Skye. I want to turn around to angle myself so I can feel the wind on my face too, to let it show me my own shape.

The other bird, the female, has landed in the field and is standing with shoulders bunched up, picking at something at her feet. A dead rabbit? A pigeon? An earthworm? There is something about seeing a bird of prey up close that loosens the limbs. It's as if there has been an exchange in the air, some lightness transferred from wing to bone. Jen points out two other kites that have appeared. Four in all. One on the ground, one in the trees and two others circling on broad wings.

This hill in Hartest is the end of the same ridge that I visited in Newmarket back in November. Ridge sounds a bit much. In reality it is a rumple, a ruck. One that starts 150 kilometres away in the Chilterns, where it is, no doubt, overshadowed by more significant hills. It was in the Chilterns that the kite was reintroduced in the 1990s by the RSPB and Natural England after the bird was persecuted to extinction in England and Scotland by gamekeepers and then taxidermists and egg collectors. I've heard it said by people around here that the ridge helped the red kites spread into Suffolk. That they followed that fold of land. I guess the air would feel different. The resistance and friction would change. I've felt something similar in water, that moment when it shifts from shallow to deep. It's a nice idea, but I guess it's more likely they followed the roads or, more accurately, the roadkill.

Half an hour later and we've drifted into the pub. We sit by a long, solid wood table next to the wide, open hearth. A log fire has been set in a grate that is raised above the red-and-black tiled floor and a soft pyramid of grey ash. We are close enough to feel the heat on the backs of our hands as we sit side on. I think of how the smoke will be bending in the wind outside. How it will be driven towards the old plane tree with its swollen trunk by the entrance of the rectory. Jen says that I look better. That I've got colour in my cheeks. She feels as if the walk and the wind have done her good too. She mentions the kites and the joy there is in such moments.

I'd been reading this morning about Wordsworth and how for him the wind was a muse and a god. At the start of the *Prelude* – his epic about his life – it was the wind that had given him life. I try to recall the words and think about how sharply Jen's eyebrows would raise if I mention it. *O there is a blessing in this gentle breeze.*

I nod. I tell her that I'd just been reading John Clare and that he'd written about kites.

> Ah, could I see a spinney nigh,
> A puddock riding in the sky
> Above the oaks with easy sail
> On stilly wings and forked tail.

She looks at me. Bet he doesn't mention they drop rabbits everywhere, she says.

MEMORY. INSPIRATION. A WUTHERING WIND.
Yorkshire, April

Memory is strange. It doesn't unfurl chronologically. It arrives in bursts in often unexpected places. I'm surprised at how many of my memories feature weather. The experience might be faded but the light remains; the blueness of a sky, the pattern of rain on the plastic cover of a pushchair. Memory feels like bubbles. Swelling with details and then popping to leave that one taste in isolation. I don't remember going to Haworth Moor in my childhood, but when I mention it in passing to my parents, they tell me we visited there as a family. It was this time of year, they say. There was snow on the ground. The wind was so sharp it went through your clothes. Cut to the bone. We didn't stay long. As soon as they mention the cold, I get a feeling of it. I do remember Brontë country. A museum. Being surprised at how little Branwell had done. I remember tiny books the size of postage stamps. Thinking how bored you would have to be to make something like that. Then the bubble pops.

Now it is me bringing my own child to Haworth Moor. Seeking out the same conditions that we turned our cheeks to. Eliza is excited about being in Brontë country. She is a child from the wrong century. Maybe it's because she is a winter baby, but she's always loved darkness. Drawn to the Gothic, the dramatic, the tragic. When I said I was going looking for a Brontë wind – a wuthering wind – she said she wanted to come. I was delighted at the idea of having company, of having one-on-one time with the second child who has always had to share us. I could almost feel the happiness fizzing off her as we drove north, listening to her chatting and singing Kate Bush with her lovely folky lilt. I tell her that I want to follow a route that the Brontës are said to have often walked. From the Parsonage where they lived, across the moor to the waterfalls. From there we will head to Top Withins, the ruins of a remote farmhouse, whose location (if not the building itself) were said to be the inspiration for the wind-lashed walls of Wuthering Heights.

It is early afternoon when we start walking. From the car we stomp the wet path that leads up onto the moor, along tracks that are wet and well trodden. Despite it being the Easter holidays, there is no one about. Eliza is not a walker. She tries, but she is sensitive. A super feeler. She feels sound and touch intensely. Tiredness and stress become physical manifestations. A cramp in the stomach. An ache in the knees, shooting pains in her heels. She hasn't walked this far for a long time and I know I will have to try to distract her as we go if we are going to make it all the way. Talking about what we can see is something that has worked before, so I challenge her to come up with descriptions as we follow the trail. I say that the heather is the colour of copper wire. She hums and haws. Sets her lips. Says, 'I think . . . cheese Doritos. No.' She thinks again, refines the images and colours. Waggles both her hands at me. 'The dust of cheese Doritos, on your fingers.'

I've been re-reading Emily Brontë's *Wuthering Heights* over the past couple of days and have been struck again by its strangeness. I'd forgotten what a spiky thing it is. Something I imagine would have had its edges knocked off if it had been published in modern times. But I've always loved the way weather is portrayed in the book. There is no separation between it and Catherine and Heathcliff. They are raised and shaped by the land and the elements, body and spirit. Cathy seems to need the wind to survive, demanding that her window should be fastened open that she be allowed 'one breath'. A passage in it reminds me too of my own walk along the Stour: when young Cathy describes the difference between her and Linton's personalities by way of their preference for a 'hot July day'. His was 'lying from morning till evening on a bank of heath in the middle of the moor'; hers was 'rocking in a rustling green tree, with a west wind blowing, and bright, white clouds flitting rapidly above'. He wanted 'peace'; 'I wanted all to sparkle and dance in a glorious jubilee.' I can't help but side with Cathy, in her thought that 'his heaven would only be half alive'.

The wind is picking up and gusting cold into our faces. We are walking into it. It is strong. Not so strong that it pushes us back, but strong enough for us to feel it in our movements. The noise of it is sharp in our ears. As if it has been honed to an edge by the grit stone. There is moisture in the air too. There will be showers today. The forecast said so, and so does the ragged bottom of the clouds. The sky is a ripped wool grey. Tomorrow, I will visit the Parsonage, the house where the Brontës lived. I will see how the hall, stairwell and landing is painted in a colour that was created from scientific analysis of pigments found in the wall. It is a grey that contains blue. Like cigarette smoke. An early visitor to the Brontës' home described it more as a 'pretty dove-coloured tint'. Looking at it will remind me of this sky; the Brontës lived among the clouds even when they were inside.

We keep walking, past grit-stone slabs and down a path that cleaves through heather that has become a darker, deeper brown. We cross Moorside Lane into a landscape that seems split in two: to the east, the wet lead of the wending path and the ragged sweep of the moor, while in the west, the verdant green of the fields, lined with parallel stripes of dry-stone walls, slope down to the river. We keep going. On past trees that have been shaped by winds so they appear perpetually blown and a farmhouse that emerges like a rocky outcrop. Another element of the Pennine to erupt from the land.

The haze of the rain grows with the wind, turning to a sleet that sticks to our faces. The path runs parallel to a wall and through the gaps we can hear ewes and lambs. They press up against it to shield themselves from the blow. The wind seems to come from everywhere – not just the west. South-west now. South. It hits us in the face, in the ears. The rooks and crows that hop around among the sheep sail on it. They are the same colour as the scraps of bin bags flapping on the barbed wire, remnants of the black plastic coverings that once covered winter silage. Eliza is tiring. She eats another Penguin, tells the joke on the back. Why did the Penguin make a pun? She pauses for me to answer. A curlew cries mournfully. Bubbling up like dark peaty water. I'm starting to associate them with wind, after hearing them on my last walk on the Stour as well. They sound as if they have the wind running through them somehow, through their binary voice box and spilling out from that beautiful curve of a beak. They are just one big vessel for it, like a bottle top or an aeolian harp. When the wind blows the curlew sings. Eliza looks at me pointedly, still waiting. For. The. Halibut. I look at her blankly and she waves the Penguin wrapper at me.

The curlew wobbles away again. We look north towards the leaden waters of the Lower Laithe Reservoir. On the other side of the wall is a horse chestnut tree that is almost unrecognisable under its crust of lichens. Old and dwarfed by the winds. We see a lapwing flapping madly. Protecting its nest maybe, or its young. The curlew keeps calling and I tell Eliza about aeolian harps, explaining that it is a type of stringed instrument that produces music whenever the wind blows across it, vibrating the strings. Coleridge had one in the window of his home that had made 'a soft floating witchery of sound'. The Romantics saw the instrument as a bridge between nature and humanity, a way for humans to see something transcendent and sublime. She listens carefully both to me and the curlew, pointing now as it flies parallel to the path, the wind under it and through it. She says it sounds like a child being struck. Like Cathy trying to get in. She sings Kate Bush again, dancing for laughs and her hair flies up and around her face as she turns with her arms in the air. I think about Catherine's words, spoken when she was ill and in bed. 'I wish I were a girl again, half savage and hardy, and free.' I take a photo for her, for future her, but also for me. Of course it is.

Because if there is one thing that weather has taught me, it is that as well as being like light, it is also intimately connected with time. According to Genesis, both weather and time were born of the same thing, the same sin. In French, their intertwined nature can still be seen in language.[13] *Les temps.* As weather passes, so does time. And, as I grow older, I realise just how fast. When you have children, you think you'll memorise every second. After all, everything they do consumes you. The noises, the expressions, even the smells in the nape of the neck, the feel of tiny fingers around your hand. But you can't keep it all. Every week, every month, your child is changed out. There is a new person in their place. Yes, some of the mannerisms will be there, some of those physical features will endure, but in ten years you haven't had one child, you've had twenty at least. When I talk to my children about when they were young, it is a different person I am describing. It is someone they don't know. That's why they are so fascinated by it, I suppose. They want to know about this person that was once in their home, in their parents' lives.

I guess I hadn't thought about it before. But now it strikes me that when my parents recalled our time on this moor, they were remembering, but also grieving. They remember more about the weather and light than that boy they once had. It's almost as if they had let go. Let him blow over the hills.

The guidebooks say prepare to share the waterfall. That it is a tourist honeypot. Today there is no one, except a young roe deer that picks its way across the other side of the beck. It's a perfect day for Emily Brontë, a woman who is portrayed as having been slightly strange and friendless. I wonder if a refusal to shun the wind and the rain might have been part of it. But Brontë's representation of the weather around Haworth, a place her sister's biographer said the 'four winds of heaven seemed to meet and rage together', was not one-dimensional. The artist Rebecca Chesney carried out a weather project in 2012 to categorise the Brontë sisters' responses to weather.[14] In *Wuthering Heights*, the wind was the most frequently mentioned. But sunshine comes a very close second. I wonder if the Brontës were similar to the Wordsworths, similar to anyone who has spent time in the elements. The moments of wonder and awe come from the transitions in the weather, when the light shifts and removes our own mortality from the shadows.

The size of the waterfall varies throughout the year. Despite the rain, today it is thin. Where the water is at its highest it flashes bone white against the bronze of the heather. It flows down from the moor, into the notch of a hanging valley. It takes its time, squiggling around stone and sliding peaty brown into the Sladen Beck. At the bottom of the falls is a seat of rock. Brontë's chair, where it's said the sisters would sit. Watch. Write. It is cold to the touch. Wet with the rain. We stand on the pack bridge that crosses the beck and look down into a small cascade in the brook, a step over which the water slides in peaty slabs. We keep going and I ask Eliza if she would like a waterfall named after her. We wonder aloud what the Brontës would think. Maybe they would be OK with the waterfall, but what about the hotel on the edge of town? What about the estate agents? The dog trainer? The gin, the Bron-tea, the engineers, the builders, the mill. Their name blown across the county.

As we start to walk up and out of the valley, Eliza stops in the path. She turns slowly, one rotation a second. She stops and calls me over, tells me to stand exactly as she is. She laughs as she marshals me, takes hold of my shoulders, puts me in position. Don't look at me, she says, it won't work. I stand staring over the moor, over the black stone walls, over the cut of Sladen Beck and the trees scaled with lichen, past the cliffs that knuckle through the moor to the heather and the dove-grey sky. We stand together. The wind sweeping our hair back, pinking our skin. The rain has hardened again; the sleet feels sharp on my face. What am I looking at? I shout the words out, but they fly back over my head like a liquid. She shouts in frustration. 'Nothing. Listen! Can't you hear it? If you stand just here . . .' She moves me again and I straighten and the wind finishes her sentence. Rushes in and over my ears. A hollow, lungless blowing. A dry hawking at the back of the throat. Wuthering is a weather word, northern in origin. Look it up and it will say: of weather, characterised by strong winds. But the word has deeper roots, maybe Scandinavian and then late Middle English. Whither. Wuther. To rush, make a rushing sound. It is a wind of urgency and passion.

The falls are almost invisible from here. Their valley, their notch in the rock, slightly darker and then gleaming with a sudden flash of white, like bone in soil, from the water. There are stone walls around us, but many have been toppled by the winds. They look old, as though they have stood for many winters before finally slumping. But there is order to their collapse too. There are numerous gaps in the wall, as if some of the stones have been cleared, used for something else. There is less heather this side of the beck. The grass is tussocks. Blond over green as if there have been highlights.

Away from the escarpment, we are so much more exposed to the wind. We walk to the crest of the hill, hands pushing on thighs, and look over the moors to where the ruins of Top Withins sit. There are trees that look as if they have grown scared. Shouted into angles by the wind. Lumps of grit stone that smoulder black. I feel good. I want to breathe it all in. But Eliza is struggling. She sits eating another Penguin, her hair stuck to her forehead. I ask if she's OK and she rallies a smile. Says she's just short of energy. But I think her feet are probably hurting, her knees too. She insists she doesn't want to turn around, says she doesn't want to spoil it, although for me, sharing this much with her has already been a treat enough. I tell her to wait and scramble up higher. Up to what looks the highest point, where the jumbled walls lie across the land like dark ribs. I stand and look east to where Top Withins lies. Sylvia Plath visited here with Ted Hughes. In his poem 'Wuthering Heights', he described how the book had become a map and when they arrived at Top Withins the farmhouse had become a 'forsaken quarry', the open moor 'all gaze'. I stand again for a second and think how the word 'gaze' seems too little for this place. That a 'look' does not capture the rush, push and raised heartbeat of this windscape. Then I turn and half run down the path towards Eliza.

The shower breaks as we leave the valley and the light sparkles over puddles. The wind is still strong, but it feels as if it is filling us now. Full of restoration. Full of a mad kind of energy. I have a feeling of lightness, like the newly well. A flit in the stomach that comes after a near miss and you realise that everything is still working. As if the body is expressing surprise or excitement at its continued functioning. As we cross Enfield Side Road, the sun glints white on puddles. Turns stone to mirror. The sky is not clear but has patches of dazzling whiteness that are teased apart to a yawn of perfect blue. The far edge of the town of Haworth is shining and over the moor is a rainbow. Eliza grips my hand tightly. We can hear the wind again now. Whirling into our ears. Making its way across the moor, through the bodies of the curlews. Leaving us with the feeling we've been moulded by the wind.

EPILOGUE

BLOSSOMING SUMMER. WEATHERED.
Felixstowe, June 2023

The sun is in the west when we get undressed and into the sea. Low enough to turn the shadows of the beach-hut roofs into narrow steeples and send them running over the sand and shingle towards the sea, but high enough to warm our backs and necks. The sky is a hard Hockney blue. Loud with colour. The light is thick and liquid. It is honey on the skin. James, Anna and Eliza are in before me. I can hear them shriek as the water reaches legs and then belly and chests. I wade after them and dive in.

Although the sea breeze is light, there is a decent swell. As I swim between the groynes, the height of the waves makes James, Anna and Eliza disappear, until they too are lifted, waving and smiling, by the waves. Further out, where the sea shallows for a spit of sand, the breakers are turning over. The sun glints on the curve of the water, turns the cement of the North Sea to something approaching blue, brightens the white crown of its crest.

We move to warm up and then just swim into the sun and hang there in the water. On shore Eliza and James take it in turns to climb onto a wooden groyne and dive back in. The sun is so bright behind them that they too become shadows. Shapes with winking edges. Eliza climbs again and I can see the glow of her, how the sun is shining on her skin and turning the water that runs down her arms and legs into sparks.

I kick out and lie on my back, basking in the feeling of the sun on my face, touching against my eyelids when they close. I remember a film that we watched a month or two ago where two students spent the winter on a beach in the Arctic Circle. They had built a shelter on volcanic black sand, had run down a snow-covered beach and surfed in water that froze on their wetsuits and gloves. At the end of the film, when the sun is finally high enough to clear the mountains and pool onto the sand, they sprint to reach it, to drink it in.

The return of the sun is welcome – but for me now, it is just one part of a vast, complex, beautiful weatherscape, and I know I need it all to experience the world to its fullest extent. The blossoming of summer is no more precious than the glimmer of ice and snow, the wild, blood-bubbling wind, the movement and beauty of an autumnal drenching.

This summer, this sun, feels as though it has crept up on us. May was unusually cool and the arrival of the heat today is almost a shock. An Iberian plume is bringing warm air from the Spanish plateau on a southerly airflow. The word 'plume' seems apt. It is a smoke signal. A warning. The memory of the record summer of 2022 still lurks. We felt it on the drive down here. The car had been sitting in the sun all day and the aircon doesn't work so we had to wind down the windows as we crawled past roadworks; the air was hot and smelt like tar. It reminded me of last year when I had to drive to work with the tyres hissing over melting roads, the bitumen spraying up onto the side of the car.

It feels as if there is less celebration, less sun worship this year. The country braced for whatever scorching temperatures this summer might bring. US scientists have confirmed that the natural weather event known as El Niño – where warm water rises to the surface and into the atmosphere – has begun in the Pacific Ocean. Its heat, they say, will likely make 2024 the world's hottest year and push the world past a key 1.5°C warming milestone. The weather can connect you to the past, ground you in the present – but also give you a glimpse to the future.

My eyes are closed but I look up under my lids. An old trick or tic, I'm not sure which, I use to break negative thoughts. If I change the direction of my eyes, my brain will change lanes, overtake the dark and disturbing. I can still hear Eliza and James. They are putting on voices, jumping, diving, splashing, repeating the jokes and catchphrases that have gathered around us. Anna is laughing, the sound rich and musical, and I open my eyes and look at them all and just then, framed in golden light, I think how beautiful life can be and then I'm laughing too, just like those boys running towards the sun on a Norwegian beach.

Afterwards we drive down the front road towards the docks that stand in an evening haze, to a street that has been made out of shipping containers. The air smells sweet. There is a throb of house music coming from a DJ. A woman whose thighs have been slapped red with sunburn dances with a boy with hair as blond as straw. We order drinks from a bar, mangling the names of the beers that have been pinned under the taps. I fidget with a white stone that I picked up from the beach. I feel the warmth of it on the skin of my fingers. Quite a few of those around us look as though they have been in the sun for more than a couple of hours; their faces glow a little too hard.

I, too, feel marked by the weather. Not from today, but over the course of this year. In some strange way, it is still in me and on me. I have been weathered.

I roll the word around. Push it against my teeth. Often we talk of weathering or being weathered in a negative way. We use it to talk of being worn, of ageing or being broken in some way. But really it is a sign of living, of viewing the world in every light, of becoming part of the rhythms of the natural world.

Since I've been writing this book, I've found that even when I'm commuting – driving the same old stretch of road day after day – I am thinking differently. Tuning in and really noticing the world around me. It sounds trite, but I'm aware of the clouds in the sky, their movements and patterns. Is that cloud receding? Is it becoming more cumulous? Is it raining over there? I notice details of the wind while I'm walking, while I'm running, while I'm swimming: the direction it is coming from; how this movement of air from some anti-cyclone in the subtropics is being shaped by the topography around me, by the topography of me.

And I hope that anyone reading this might also be encouraged to look again at weather, to become immersed in it and to discover that there can be beauty and wonder and fun in every flake, drop and gust.

ACKNOWLEDGEMENTS

This book would have been impossible without the generosity, support and encouragement from a number of people. Thank you to:

Natalie Goodbrand, Annie Vincent, Emma Blois, Megan Tuckwood, Caroline Anderson, Freya Dean and everyone who sails in the good ship Spicer Wing. Thank you also to Jonathan Russell for allowing me the time off to write this book; I am very grateful.

Megan Reynard for her endless support and to Nicola Eley, Bethany Warner and the rest of the team (Pauline, Emma, Bec, Katie, Lex, Charlotte) who endured me moaning through the edits with good grace.

My friends James and Anna, for coming with us to Scotland and showing us just how much fun can be had in any weather. Big love.

Shaun Norris, Olly Clanford and Will Cranstoun. No way there are five sixes.

Jonny (for the jokes), Martin, Paul, Kate, Andy, Sean and countless others for always asking on the sidelines how the book was going. Come on you Rams.

The team at Elliott & Thompson, who have been unwavering in their support and kindness. Thanks in particular to Pippa who endured my latest simile obsession and need to 'think' with a saintly patience.

Isabel Vogel, who again helped me navigate first drafts of the book with insight and kindness.

My family.

My mum and dad, who have always done everything they could to support me.

Seth and Eliza, who (sort of) allowed me to write about them and who I am so, so proud of.

Lyra, who still HATES every form of weather.

And, of course, thank you to Jen for always being there, whatever the weather. I love you and I promise that 'book Jen' is definitely not a 'bitch'.

NOTES

Rain

1. Melissa Harrison, *Rain* (Faber & Faber, 2016)
2. Cloud Appreciation Society, https://cloudappreciationsociety. org/cloud-library/pannus/
3. F. Bocci, 'Whether or not to run in the rain', *European Journal of Physics*, vol. 33, no. 5 (2012)
4. J. B. MacKinnon, *The Once and Future World* (Vintage Canada, 2014)
5. ibid.
6. D. Q. Andrews, T. Stoiber, A. M. Temkin, O. V. Naidenko, 'Discussion. Has the human population become a sentinel for the adverse effects of PFAS contamination on wildlife health and endangered species?', *Science of the Total Environment*, 2023
7. William Wordsworth, *Guide to the Lakes* (Oxford Paperbacks, 1977)
8. Dorothy Wordsworth, *Journals of Dorothy Wordsworth: Volume I & II Complete* (Independent, 2021)
9. A. Harris, *Weatherland: Writers & Artists Under English Skies* (Thames & Hudson, 2015)
10. L. Jones, *Losing Eden* (Penguin, 2020)

Fog

1. www.metoffice.gov.uk
2. J. C. Culham, 'Motion perception: New ideas on how drivers perceive speed emerge from the fog', eLife (2012)
3. R. Burton, *The Anatomy of Melancholy* (New York Review Classics, 2001)
4. W. H. Te Brake, 'Air pollution and fuel crises in preindustrial London, 1250–1650', *Technology and Culture*, vol. 16 (1975)
5. Harris, *Weatherland*
6. M. L. Bell and D. L. Davis, 'Reassessment of the lethal London fog of 1952: novel indicators of acute and chronic consequences of acute exposure to air pollution', *Environ Health Perspect*, vol. 109 (June 2001)
7. E. Killam, *The Detection of Human Remains* (Charles C. Thomas Publisher, 2004)
8. Lilla Lovász, Antoine Fages and Valentin Amrhein, 'Konik, Tarpan, European wild horse: An origin story with conservation implications', *Global Ecology and Conservation*, vol. 32 (2021)
9. S. T. Coleridge, 'Constancy to an Ideal Object' (1828)

Wind

1. L. Watson, *Heaven's Breath* (William Morrow & Co., 1985)
2. M. A. Mohammad, S. Koul, R. Rylance, et al., 'Association of weather with day-to-day incidence of myocardial infarction: A SWEDEHEART nationwide observational study', *JAMA Cardiol*, vol. 3, no. 11 (2018)
3. F. G. Sulman, A. Danon, Y. Pfeifer, et al., 'Urinalysis of patients suffering from climatic heat stress (Sharav)', *Int J Biometeorol*, vol. 14 (1970)
4. Watson, *Heaven's Breath*
5. Claude E. Benson, 'The Helm Wind', The Yorkshire Ramblers' Club, https://www.yrc.org.uk/journal-and-image-archive/journal-selector/yrc-journal-1911-vol-3-no-11/journal-v3n11p239/
6. Amelia Soth, 'Madness on the wind', *JSTOR Daily*, 6 July 2023
7. W. James, *The Principles of Psychology* (Dover, 2000)

8. Tim Ingold, 'The eye of the storm: Visual perception and the weather', *Visual Studies*, vol. 20 (2005)
9. https://www.pnas.org/doi/10.1073/pnas.1402786111
10. W. H. Hudson, *Birds and Man* (Read Books, 2001)
11. J. Muir, *John Muir: Nature Writings* (Library of America, 1984)
12. N. Hunt, *Where the Winds Are* (Nicholas Brealey Publishing, 2017)
13. Harris, *Weatherland*
14. Harris, *Weatherland*

INDEX